UNIVERSITY OF NORTH CAROLINA AT CHAPEL HILL
DEPARTMENT OF ROMANCE LANGUAGES

NORTH CAROLINA STUDIES
IN THE ROMANCE LANGUAGES AND LITERATURES

Founder: URBAN TIGNER HOLMES

Distributed by:

UNIVERSITY OF NORTH CAROLINA PRESS

CHAPEL HILL
North Carolina 27514
U.S.A.

NORTH CAROLINA STUDIES IN THE
ROMANCE LANGUAGES AND LITERATURES

Number 209

"DUEÑAS" AND *"DONCELLAS"*:
A STUDY OF THE "DOÑA RODRÍGUEZ" EPISODE IN *"DON QUIJOTE"*

"DUEÑAS" AND *"DONCELLAS"*:

A Study of the "Doña Rodríguez" Episode in *"Don Quijote"*

BY

CONCHITA HERDMAN MARIANELLA

CHAPEL HILL

NORTH CAROLINA STUDIES IN THE ROMANCE
LANGUAGES AND LITERATURES
U.N.C. DEPARTMENT OF ROMANCE LANGUAGES
1979

Library of Congress Cataloging in Publication Data

Marianella, Conchita Herdman.
  "Dueñas" and "doncellas."

(North Carolina studies in the Romance languages and literatures; no. 209)
Bibliography: p.
  1. Cervantes Saavedra, Miguel de, 1547-1616. Don Quixote. 2. Cervantes
Saavedra, Miguel de, 1547-1616 — Characters — Women. 3. Cervantes Saavedra, Miguel de, 1547-1616 — Characters — Doña Rodríguez. 4. Women in
literature. I. Title. II. Series.

PQ6353.M36   863'.3   79-10353
ISBN 0-8078-9209-2

I. S. B. N. 0-8078-9209-2

IMPRESO EN ESPAÑA

PRINTED IN SPAIN

DEPÓSITO LEGAL: V. 1.355 - 1979   I. S. B. N. 84-499-2749-8

ARTES GRÁFICAS SOLER, S. A. - JÁVEA, 28 - VALENCIA (8) - 1979

ACKNOWLEDGMENTS

I wish to express my deep appreciation to Professor Luis A. Murillo for his thoughtful guidance and critical discussions, and to Professors Edwin S. Morby and Joseph J. Duggan for a careful reading and criticisms of the manuscript. I also wish to thank Professor Dorothy C. Shadi for making available selective references. I am grateful to the Department of Spanish and Portuguese, University of California, Berkeley, for my appointment to the Charles E. Kany Graduate Scholarship, as a result of which I was able to devote a full year to the initial research for this work.

TABLE OF CONTENTS

CHAPTER I

PRELIMINARY

The ladies and damsels of the phrase *'dueñas y doncellas'* are remembered principally as the gracious, beautiful and noble women of chivalric romance. Although the phrase appears in Castilian literature from the early Middle Ages, we are most familiar with *'dueñas y doncellas'* as literary and traditional figures in the fifteenth- and sixteenth-century prose romances, where they are noble ladies-in-waiting attending to their ladies and to visiting knights. The *doncellas*, deriving mainly from the damsels of the French Arthurian romances — fair, noble, wise, clever and prudent — were idealized and romanticized figures. As depicted in the *libros de caballerías*, they wandered on the roads and in forests on palfreys, in the service of their ladies or for personal reasons. Wandering *doncellas* often found themselves "in distress," and would be rescued from their predicament at the timely moment by knights-errant. Other noble *doncellas* remained at court or in castles and palaces. Confidantes to their ladies, they often served as intermediaries, carrying messages to the favored knight and even arranging nocturnal meetings for their lady and her knight. We could say that our *doncellas* were ideally suited to the narratives of both deeds of arms and erotic encounters of adventurous knights.

Dueñas were also noble attendants in the romances, but as such they tended to remain background figures. Since they were often older, widowed women, activities like those of the *doncellas* must not have been considered proper for them. They were not romantic figures. Rather, it is the *dueña de gran guisa*, the lady of estate, who has a more prominent role. The *dueña menesterosa*, a role played by the *dueña de gran guisa*, is a conspicuous figure of Castilian chivalric romance. Like the counterpart "*doncella*-in-distress," these ladies were in frequent need of knights' aid, with the difference that, while the *doncellas* needed succor in defense of life and honor, the *dueñas* need it in defense of family and property. Although many *dueñas de gran guisa* were beautiful and possessed all the courtly qualities, they were not given in Castilian literature the same traits as *doncellas*. They appear as women in a certain plight, and their role is more restricted.

The *dueñas* and *doncellas* of the Castilian romances derive from the '*dames et damoiseles*' of the French romances. The original figures or models of the *damoiseles* were, in many respects, courtly re-creations of folkloric and mythological figures. Although the roles of *dames* and *damoiseles* in the French romances were not, and could not be identical, if only because of age and marital status, the differences between them were less dramatic than in Castilian literature. For instance, a French *dame* could have an affair with a knight even if she were married, a turn of events most unlikely in the Castilian prose romances. What could account for this evident divergence in the roles of *dueñas* and *doncellas*? A look into the earliest appearances of the figures in Castilian literature will reveal that *dueñas* and *doncellas* do not share to the same degree a common derivation from the French Arthurian romances. When the Arthurian legends were first rendered into Castilian the acceptable equivalents for French *dame* and *damoisele* already existed in peninsular traditions. *Dueñas* and *doncellas* appear in documents and in literature as early as the twelfth and thirteenth centuries. The *dueñas* of the *Cantar de mío Cid*, not yet further differentiated by the term *dueñas* and *doncellas*, served as attendants to Doña Jimena and her daughters. We find "dueñas y doncellas" mentioned as part of the royal household in the *Siete Partidas*,[1] where the coupling refers to actual ladies-in-

---

[1] *Las siete partidas del rey don Alfonso el Sabio,* Partida II, Título XIV, Ley III, v. 2, Real Academia de la Historia (Madrid, 1807), p. 129: *Cómo debe el pueblo guardar al rey en las dueñas, et en las doncellas et en las otras mugeres que andan en casa de la reyna.*

Cámara llamaron antiguamente la casa de la reyna, ca bien asi como en la cámara han a ser las cosas que hi ponen encobiertas et guardadas, asi las dueñas et las doncellas que andan en casa de la reyna deben seer apartadas e guardadas de vista et de baldonamiento de malos homes et de malas mugeres, et esto por tres razones: la primera por honra e por guarda del rey et de la reyna, la segunda por honra dellas mismas, la tercera por honra de sus parientes...

waiting of royalty. This term, used to refer to social figures, provided a suitable vehicle for the translation of fictional *dames* and *damoiseles*. In Castile *dueñas* and *doncellas* were both social and literary figures quite early. There seems to have been a slight adaptation of the literary *dueñas* and *doncellas* to the social ones. While the *doncellas* derive directly from the *damoiseles* of the French romances, the figure of the *dueña* as a rule is colored more by the reality of her role in medieval Castilian society than by a recollection of the role of the fictional *dames* of Arthurian romance. The *dueñas* of the Castilian prose romances were more concerned with the maintenance of family, property and authority than with romantic attachments.

Dueñas and *doncellas* appear in *Don Quijote,* Parts I and II. '*Dueñas y doncellas*' was initially, as in the *Cid* and the *Siete Partidas,* a phrase designating ladies-in-waiting. We find *dueñas* and *doncellas* from early times as both social and literary figures. In the prose romances, from the early *Caballero Cifar* to the late *Palmerín de Inglaterra,* they appear as figures in certain traditional situations, and the roles they play individually are topical. When we read of Elisena's or Oriana's being accompanied by '*dueñas y doncellas*' in *Amadís de Gaula,* the phrase refers to noble attendants. These ladies are typical figures in traditional situations. '*Dueñas y doncellas*' so coupled are always mentioned as being present at scenes of the arrival and departure of an illustrious personage from a castle. The situations they appear in when they are dealt with individually — *doncella*-in-distress, intermediary *doncella,* enamored *doncella, dueña menesterosa* — are topics of the prose romances. *Dueñas* and *doncellas,* however, are a theme for Cervantes, and the treatment he gives it is subtle and complex. Although Cervantes parodies certain situations of the prose romances, such as the ones we have just mentioned, in which *dueñas* and *doncellas* appear, he ultimately deals with the social figures of his own time.

We will examine in this dissertation the treatment Cervantes gives to '*dueñas y doncellas*,' proceeding from a study of the situations of the prose romances he parodies to his depiction of them in *Don Quijote*. We will eventually be dealing with the theme of *dueñas* and *doncellas* in *Don Quijote* and principally with the Doña Rodríguez episode of 1615. Chapter II begins with a brief examination of the etymology of *dueña, doña* and *dama,* as a prelude to a study of literary *dueñas* and *doncellas* in Castilian literature prior to Cervantes.

The figures as well as the situations and topics they appear in will be studied, from the *Cantar de mío Cid* to *Palmerín de Inglaterra* (1547), where the slightest change of emphasis begins to intrude into the traditional depiction. Chapter III is concerned with the *dueña* of contemporary society — the social figure — as she appeared in the works of Cervantes, Mateo Alemán, Suárez de Figueroa and Quevedo. Chapter IV deals with the theme of *dueñas* and *doncellas* in *Don Quijote*, Parts I and II, and Chapter V with the Doña Rodríguez episode.

The phrase '*dueñas y doncellas*' preserved the medieval and archaic connotations from its use in the *libros de caballerías* even in the social life of Cervantes' time. In his stylistic use of it, he consciously sets out to contrast those connotations with the contemporary meaning. "Dueñas" and "doncellas" were servants in Spanish homes in the sixteenth and seventeenth centuries, and the phrase, as used both in social life and in literature, described these contemporary figures of society. Cervantes juxtaposes figures drawn from contemporary life with figures recollected from the pages of chivalric literature. The phrase appears in his description of Don Quijote's departure from the ducal palace:

> ... Saliendo don Quijote, habiéndose despedido la noche antes de los duques, una mañana se presentó armado en la plaza del castillo. Mirábanle de los corredores toda la gente del castillo, y asimismo los duques salieron a verle ... Estando mirándolos todos, a deshora, *entre las otras dueñas y doncellas* de la duquesa, alzó la voz la desenvuelta y discreta Altisidora. ... [2]

We noted that in medieval documents '*dueñas y doncellas*' had referred to specific persons and situations. It is used in the *Siete Partidas* to describe actual ladies-in-waiting to royalty. In the romances it had referred to noble attendants, and these were traditionally depicted as being present at scenes of arrival and departure. However, in the scene described above, the *dueñas* and *doncellas* mentioned are mere contemporary servants brought forth by Cervantes to stand

---

[2] Miguel de Cervantes, *Don Quijote de la Mancha*, ed. Martín de Riquer (Barcelona: Editorial Planeta, 1968), II.57.1011-1012. (Italics mine.) Subsequent references to the text of *Don Quijote* are to this edition, unless otherwise stated. Quotations will be followed by part (I or II), chapter and page.

in contrast to the idealized figures of chivalric romance. In the course of the sixteenth century both terms had acquired a modern or contemporary denotation that made various new connotations possible. One of the most obvious was *dueña* as 'go-between.'

Dueñas and *doncellas* was not one of the major themes Cervantes set out to parody when he conceived his story of the *ingenioso hidalgo* in the final decade of the sixteenth century. He was interested then primarily in the parody of what we might term "male" situations, deeds of arms and valor typical of the knight, that would apply directly to Don Quijote. Concomitantly, in the process of creating his character and the contemporary life around him, he came upon the situations most pleasing to him, and to these he dedicated the full resource of his mature wit and art of delineating character. This is the Doña Rodríguez episode, where he expanded a theme both literary and social into a situation of great novelistic promise that merged literature and life. He portrays Doña Rodríguez as a real *dueña* of contemporary society who confuses her identity with the *dueñas* of an archaic literary mode.

The social portrait of the *dueña* in the *Quijote* of 1615 has an unusual significance. The figure of the *dueña* in the literature of the late sixteenth and seventeenth centuries is largely restricted to the novel and satirical prose, where she is ridiculed and censured. The *dueña de servicio* is depicted as she was observed in contemporary society — a necessary but much disliked servant in the homes of the wealthy and noble. The depiction of this old woman, from its earliest appearance in the last years of the sixteenth century, is more of an exposure than a portrait, for she had become popularized to the degree that her negative qualities could be enlarged into caricature. The modern *dueña* is portrayed in the works of Cervantes and his contemporaries as a cross, bothersome and complaining old woman. By far the most serious accusation leveled against her was that she acted as a go-between. Present in the home to protect the honor and safety of the young ladies and unmarried servants, this servant of authority, dressed in her severe traditional garb — a symbol of her authority — is depicted as an unscrupulous, calculating *medianera,* working her treachery for financial gain, or for even more shameful reasons. Cervantes in particular censured the *dueña* for such behavior with indignation, and it is in his works that we find the most complete picture of her negative qualities. For his depiction of the *dueña* he draws not on literature, but on life — the society around him.

One may seek in vain a satisfactory explanation for this picture of the *dueña*. To what degree the social group was innocent or guilty of such serious wrongdoing as *tercería* we may never know. In the course of our investigation, however, we shall perforce confront certain questions. Were *dueñas* entirely blameless as a group or was there some basis in fact for the literary depiction? Is there a possible antecedent in Spanish literature that might account for the rapid proliferation (at the close of the sixteenth century) of the figure of this old woman as a *tercera* with overwhelmingly negative traits? Might we conjecture that at least initially the Celestina type figure had some influence on the literary portrayal of the *dueña*?

Although the portrait of the *dueña* we find in many authors is a stereotype, she becomes a full character in Cervantes' hands. The *dueña* Doña Rodríguez, coping with life's real problems out of a limited understanding of surrounding reality, is a full-bodied character even while typifying on one level the negative qualities ascribed to the figure of the *dueña*. A particular set of circumstances and her own foolishness combine to induce her to re-enact the literary role of *dueña menesterosa*, totally unaware that she is doing so. A real *dueña* unwittingly imitates a literary *dueña*, thereby confusing literature and life and sealing her own fate. The path from literary *dueñas* and *doncellas* to real *dueñas* and *doncellas* is a long one, and it is in fact Cervantes' creative genius that imposes the connection — the thematic relation — upon us by his merger of life and art.

CHAPTER II

DUEÑAS AND DONCELLAS IN SPANISH LITERATURE
PRIOR TO CERVANTES, A SURVEY

I. Etymology

It may prove helpful to begin with a brief etymological sketch of the word 'dueña.' 'Dueña' (< Lat. 'dŏmĭna'), the tonic noun meaning 'señora' (lady) and atonic 'doña,' the title of respect, can be traced in hispano-romance to the early eleventh century. [1] Menéndez Pidal gives an example of a special emphatic usage found in an eleventh-century document: "illa *duanna donna* Urraca, illa *dona donna* Urraka." [2] The meaning is "la señora doña Urraca." [3] When the title appears alone, the form may sometimes be stressed, with resultant diphthongization. [4]

---

[1] "Don" may be used before a feminine name beginning with a vowel. In the *Cid* we find "don Elvira" and in Berceo, "don Oria."

[2] Ramón Menéndez Pidal, *Orígenes del español, Obras completas* (Madrid, 1934-1953), v. 8, p. 328. The example is from †1062 San Juan de la Peña.

[3] J. Corominas, *Diccionario crítico etimológico de la lengua castellana* (Bern, 1954). Menéndez Pidal, *Orígenes,* attributes the use of this emphatic form to feminine vanity:

> En mis documentos, salvo el caso de las Glosas Emilianenses, no hallo este doble antepuesto a nombres de hombre, ni siquiera tratándose de los más encumbrados señores que gobernaban el reino aragonés. Parece que era un uso propio principal para halagar la vanidad femenina. No todas las señoras tomaban el doble *domna*: los documentos lo dan constantemente a unas y lo niegan a otras; en nuestro documento de +1062 SJ Peña se ve claramente que "illa duanna donna Urraka," llamada así varias veces, es señora de más campanillas que las que siempre se llaman simplemente "donna Adulina" o "donna Sanga" (329).

[4] "Por lo demás, el simple título, cuando va solo, lleva a menudo diptongo, propio de evolución como palabra acentuada 'duanne Ezo, duanna Adu-

Throughout the Middle Ages *dueña* continued to refer to 'noble lady,' or merely to 'woman' (in general) or 'wife.' [5] In twelfth-century Castile we find 'dueña' = 'lady' with reference to both married and unmarried ladies (Doña Jimena, but also Don [Doña] Elvira and Doña Sol). *Dueñas*, additionally, were ladies-in-waiting. It seems clear that a woman who may be called 'dueña' (lady) is also entitled to the title of respect 'doña.' We find thirteenth-century examples of 'dueña' meaning 'women in general,' as in Berceo's *Milagros*: "Nunqua varon en duenna metió maior querencia." [6] The Virgin is referred to as *duenna* (357d, 358a, 529a). [7] Another example from Berceo will show that in the thirteenth century 'dueña' could still be applied to unmarried women:

> Enpeçaron las uirgines lazradas a sobir,
> Enpeçolas la duen[n]a reclusa a segujr;
> Quando don Oria cato Dios lo qujso conplir,
> Fue puyada en somo por uerdat uos dezir . . .

> Estas quatro donzellas ligeras mas que biento
> Obieron con este arbol plazer e pagamjento;
> … … … … … … … … … … … … … …
> Estando enel arbor estas duennas contadas
> … … … … … … … … … … … … … …
> Vieron enel çielo finjestras foradadas . . . [8]

Clearly, in these strophes *donzella* is a synonym for *virgen* and *duenna* may be used interchangeably with *donzella*. It is also Berceo who presents us with the first documented use of *dama* in Spanish, [9] as a noun referring to the Virgin: "esti es nuestro Sire, e nuestra Dama." [10] The influence would seem to be French. *Dama* is not an indigenous derivation from *dŏmĭna*.

---

lina,' en el mismo documento de SJ Peña". Menéndez Pidal, *Orígenes*, 328 (note).

[5] Ralph Steele Boggs, *et al.*, *Tentative Dictionary of Medieval Spanish* (Chapel Hill, 1946).

[6] Gonzalo de Berceo, *Milagros de nuestra señora*, ed. A. G. Solalinde, Clás. Cast., 1964, p. 13, stanza 50b.

[7] Nuns may be called *dueña* also, as in *Milagros*, 567b or 561b.

[8] *La vida de Santa Oria, Cuatro poemas de Berceo*, ed. C. Carroll Marden (Madrid, 1928), pp. 77-78, strophes 41, 45 and 46 respectively.

[9] Corominas, *Dic. crít. etim.*, s.v. *dama*.

[10] *Milagros*, p. 151, 650b.

The usage of *dueña* = lady continues throughout the Middle Ages, and, even in the fourteenth century, 'dueña' may mean 'woman in general,' as in the title of the Arcipreste's poem "De las propiedades que las dueñas chicas han." By the fifteenth century we begin to see evidence of the word's displacement in the sense of 'lady' by 'dama' (< French 'dame'). 'Damas' now appears to be used as a term inclusive of 'dueñas' and 'doncellas.' The opening lines of the ballad of "Lanzarote" are:

> Nvnca fuera cauallero
> de damas tan bien seruido
> como fuera Lançarote
> quando de Bretaña vino
> que dueñas curauan del
> donzellas del su rocino . . .[11]

In the *Cancionero de Baena* (1445) *dama* is occasionally used as a synonym for *dueña*. [12] For instance, in Villasandino's "Cantiga" no. 17 we find:

> As donçellas denle onor
> a esta noble flor de lys,
> e damas d'este pays
> loan su pres e loor: . . .

Dama may be found in the poems of the Marqués de Santillana or Jorge Manrique. In Santillana's "Villancico a tres fijas suyas" we read:

> Por una gentil floresta
> de lindas flores e rosas
> vide tres damas fermosas
> que de amores han recuesta [13]

and in strophe 17 of Manrique's *Coplas*:

---

[11] *Cancionero de romances (Amberes, 1550)*, ed. A. Rodríguez-Moñino (Madrid, 1967), pp. 283-284.

[12] See *Cancionero de Juan Alfonso de Baena*, ed. José María Azáceta (Madrid, 1966), no. 18 (variant), no. 41 (rubric) and no. 572 (variant).

[13] *Marqués de Santillana: canciones y decires*, ed. Vicente García de Diego, Clás. Cast., 1964, p. 214.

¿Qué fizieron las damas
sus tocados, sus vestidos,
sus olores? [14]

It seems safe to say that by at least 1550, in poetic usage, as well as social, 'dama' has completely replaced 'dueña' in the acceptation of 'lady.' 'Dueña' would no longer mean 'lady' primarily, and its usage in this sense would be restricted to the romances of chivalry, where it would stand in isolation. Likewise, 'dueña' in the acceptation of 'woman' would be found only in rustic speech of archaic tendency. [15] Perhaps 'dueña' became so closely associated with the idea of "waiting lady" that it could no longer be synonymous with "lady." From this point the term became increasingly restricted, and finally came to designate the servant of Spanish homes, the *dueña de servicio.*

Latin 'dŏmĭna' did not follow the same path in France or Italy as it did in Spain, the cause being, of course, the differences in conditions under which diphthongization occurs in these countries. The diphthongization of V.L. ǫ and ę under stress in a closed romance syllable (leading to tonic *dueña* and atonic *doña*) is a Castilian peculiarity. In France 'dŏmĭna' gave 'dame,' both noun (= lady) and title. The word was used substantially the same way in France as the corresponding term in Spain. A *dame* was a married lady, or any lady of estate, married or unmarried. [16] In the eleventh century we

---

[14] Comparing Manrique's usage to F. Sánchez Talavera's "Desir [de las vanidades del mundo], *Canc. de Baena,* no. 530, we find in the older poet the following:

3   ¿Qué se fizieron los emperadores
. . .
4   ¿Padres e fijos, hermanos, parientes,
amigos, amigas, que mucho amamos,
con quien comimos, bevimos, folgamos,
muchas garridas e fermosas gentes,
dueñas, doncellas, mancebos valientes.

[15] Cervantes was aware of this usage. In one of the cases brought before Sancho as governor, a woman accuses a "ganador rico" of rape. The man refers to his accuser as "esta buena dueña" (II.45.922). The meaning is 'mujer.' The story would seem to be a folk tale preserving rustic usage.

[16] "Dame — 1) titre qu'on donnait à la femme d'un seigneur, d'un châtelain, d'un chevalier... par opposition aux femmes mariées de la bourgeoisie qui ont porté pendant longtemps le nom de demoiselles..." and "titre qu'on donnait à la femme qui possédait une seigneurie," and also "la femme noble à laquelle un chevalier consacrait ses soins" *Dictionnaire de la langue fran-*

find *dame* in the *Chanson de Roland* in the sense of noblewoman: "Ne a muiler ne a dame qu'aies veüd / N'en vanteras el regne dont tu fus." [17] The troubadours conferred connotations of love-service to *dompna* and *mi dons* which eventually influenced the chivalric tradition. Guillaume IX d'Aquitaine, in "Mout jauzens me prenc en amar," writes

> Toutz joys li deu humiliar,
> Et tota ricors obezir
> Mi dons, per son belh aculhir
> E per son belh plazent esguar ... [18]

and in "Farai chansoneta nueva"

> Et no m'en tengatz per yure
> S'ieu ma bona dompna am ... (20).

In the twelfth century Chrétien de Troyes uses *dame* in the sense of lady (noun and title). *La dame de Noauz,* a lady of high rank, sponsors a tournament in *Le Chevalier de la Charrete.*

> ... s'anpristrent a cel parlemant
> une ahatine et un tornoi.
> Vers celi de Pomelegoi
> l'anprist la dame de Noauz. [19]

'Dame' is also applied to the Senescal's wife, who gives Lancelot temporary freedom to attend the tournament (p. 166, l. 5437). The tournament is attended, of course, by many *dames* and *damoiseles*:

> Dames et dameiseles gentes
> I rot tant que mervoille fu
> (168.5524-5525).

çaise, ed. E. Littré (Paris, 1874). Littré traces the history of the word from the eleventh century to the fifteenth in a thumbnail sketch, with examples from authors. See also "domina," Walther von Wartburg, *Französisches Etymologisches Wörterbuch.*

[17] *La Chanson de Roland,* ed. Joseph Bédier [252nd edition of Paris, 1937], Paris, 1964, CXLVI, p. 164, 1.1960-1961.

[18] *Les chansons de Guillaume IX, Duc d'Aquitaine* (1071-1127), ed. Alfred Jeanroy (Paris, 1913), pp. 22-23, l. 19-22.

[19] *Les romans de Chrétien de Troyes,* v. 3, *Le Chevalier de la Charrete,* ed. Mario Roques (Paris, 1967), p. 163, l. 5366-5367.

In the *Vulgate Lancelot* Guinevere is consistently called "dame" in direct address, and noblewomen, such as Lady Mallehault, are "dame." [20] Lore of Carduel is called "damoisele" when mentioned, but also "Dame Lore," as a title (258, l. 12). Grail damsels are "damoiseles" (v. 5, Part III, p. 108, l. 11). The idea of service to the *dame*, begun by the troubadours, is found in Chrétien, of course, and continued in the *Vulgate Lancelot*. A Latin precedent was Ovid's use of *domina*, as in *Ars Amatoria*, for instance: "Arbitrio dominae tempora perde tua" (I.504). [21] French 'dame,' as presented in these romances, is not translated into Castilian as "dama" (the later derivation) through the fifteenth century, but as "dueña." For instance, the Castilian prose *Lancelot* (1414) speaks of "la dueña de Malagud." Seventeenth-century Fr. *duègne* is a late borrowing from the Spanish.

Italian 'dònna' (thirteenth century), also, derives from 'dŏmĭna,' and has a similar usage as in the other romance languages. [22] We find in Dante:

> Poscia ch'io ebbi il mio dottore udito
> nomar le donne antiche e'caualieri,
> pietà mi guinse, e fui quasi smarrito. [23]

The term 'dama,' a French borrowing as in the Spanish, is found early in Italian. In the fourteenth-century *Tavola Ritonda* we read, for example, "La Dama del Lago" (title) or "nella compagnía di su dama e di trenta cavalieri" (noun). [24] 'Dama' is used here as a synonym of the more usual 'dònna.'

---

[20] *Le livre de Lancelot del Lac, Vulgate Version*, ed. H. O. Sommer (Washington, D.C., 1908-1916), III, Part I, p. 257, l. 40.

[21] James J. Wilhelm, *The Cruelest Month: Spring, Nature, and Love in Classical and Medieval Lyrics* (New Haven, 1965), writes "Ovid developed the notion of the beloved as *domina* ('lady or mistress of the heart'). The Latin word was applied to the wives of plantation owners, who became the dukes of medieval estates, and the great ladies of the Roman aristocracy" (Appendix, p. 271).

[22] See *Dizionario Etimologico Italiano*, ed. Carlo Battisti and Giovanni Alessio (Florence, 1967).

[23] *La Divina Commedia, Inferno*, ed. Natalino Sapegno (Florence, 1967), I.5.71.

[24] See *La Tavola Ritonda o L'istoria di Tristano, Collezione di Opere Inedite o Rare*, v. 10, ed. F.-L. Polidori (Bologna, 1864), Chap. VI, p. 13, for both examples. The *Lexicon* deals extensively with the meaning of 'dama' in the text, as both title and noun (v. 11, pp. 53-54). It is given as a synonym of 'dònna.'

II. *Cantar de mío Cid*

The figure of the *dueña* appears in Spanish literature as early as the *Cantar de mío Cid*, where, however, the word 'doncella' is not used. 'Dueña' has two clear applications in the Castilian poem, referring to 1) noble ladies and young girls and to 2) attendants or ladies-in-waiting. [25] It thus includes both married and unmarried women, who in subsequent works are further identified as *dueñas* and *doncellas*. Doña Jimena and her daughters are called *dueña*, a term of respect. The title for all three is *doña*. The acceptation, of course, is "noblewomen." For example, King Alfonso entrusts the three ladies to Minaya using the following words:

> yo les mandaré dar conducho — mientra que por mi tierra foren,
> de fonta e de mal — curiallas e de deshonore;
> quando en cabo de mi tierra — aquestas dueñas foren,
> catad cómmo las sirvades — vos e el campeadore. [26]

Similarly, when Minaya Álbar Fáñez gives the hand of Doña Elvira and Doña Sol to the Infantes de Carrión, he says "dovos estas dueñas - amas son fijas dalgo" (II.111.2232). The usage in this sense is constant. [27]

Nonetheless, *dueña* in the *Cid* in more frequently used in its second acceptation (lady-in-waiting), indicating Doña Jimena's attendants. In their first appearance in the poem they hold the Cid's daughters in their arms. The author describes the arrival of Doña Jimena to bid her husband farewell:

---

[25] Although Menéndez Pidal, *Cantar de mío Cid, texto, gramática y vocabulario* (Madrid, 1911), II, p. 632, and also Boggs, 201, term the *dueñas* who attend to Doña Jimena and her daughters "dueñas de servicio," I would prefer to describe them as "dueñas de honor." The *dueña de servicio* is a servant of comparatively humbler origin than the lady-in-waiting, and would not warrant the attention given *dueñas* in the *Cid*. Furthermore, the *dueña de servicio* is generally a widow, or an unmarried older woman. In the *Cid*, the term 'dueña' encompasses what would later be broken down into "dueñas" and "doncellas," ladies-in-waiting to more noble ladies.

[26] *Poema de mío Cid*, ed. Ramón Menéndez Pidal, Clás. Cast., 1913, II.82.1356-1359. Subsequent references will include, as here, *cantar, canto* and line number(s).

[27] I find at least seven occasions where *dueña* clearly applies to the Cid's wife and daughters, and twelve references to the attendant *dueñas*. See *Voc.*, 632 for Menéndez Pidal's observations on the usage of 'dueña.'

> Afevos doña Ximena — con sus fijas do va llegando;
> señas dueñas las traen — e adúzenlas en los braços.
> Ant el Campeador doña Ximena — fincó los inojos amos...
>
> (I.15.262-264).

The *dueñas'* duties are to serve Doña Jimena. When the Cid departs
from Valencia to be reconciled with Alfonso, he leaves his family
behind, with instructions to his men for their safety:

> Las puertas del alcáçer — mio Çid lo mandó,
> que non se abriessen — de día nin de noch;
> dentro es su mugier — e sus fijas amas a dos,
> en que tiene su alma — e so coraçon,
> e otras dueñas — que las sirven a su sabor...
>
> (II.104.2002-2005).

It is evident that the "otras dueñas" form an important part of
the Cid's household (Menéndez Pidal, *Cid*, v. 2, 632). They receive
every consideration from him and Doña Jimena. They are provided
for along with his wife and daughters when the Cid goes into exile
(I.15.252-254). They seem to lend status or prestige to the lady they
serve, for Doña Jimena constantly refers to them; it appears that
they form part of the frame of reference for her identity as a noblewoman. Asking for the Cid's good counsel, she says to him:

> Fem ante vos — yo e vuestras ffijas,
> iffantes son — e de días chicas,
> con aquestas mis dueñas — de quien so yo servida.
>
> ... ...
> Dandnos consejo — por amor de santa María!
>
> (I.16.269-273).

When Doña Jimena's *dueñas* prepare to accompany her to a reunion
with the Cid, Minaya sees to it that they are richly dressed and
mounted on fine mules and palfreys so that their category will be
evident ("que non parescan mal" [II.83.1428]). After the second battle
of Valencia, the Cid proves to his own family and to the Castilians
his growing prestige and wealth by honoring his wife's *dueñas*:

> Ya mugier doña Ximena, — nom lo aviedes rogado?
> Estas dueñas que aduxiestes, — que vos sirven tanto,
> quiérolas casar — con de aquestos míos vassallos;

a cada una dellas — doles dozientos marcos,
que lo sepan en Castiella, — a quién sirvieron tanto
(II.95.1763-1767). [28]

The *dueña* is not a figure of relief in the *Cid*. The *dueñas* who are attendants are not described, and do not have speaking roles. However, it is important that *dueñas* are seen to hold a necessary and honorable position in the home of a nobleman. Their presence confirms the prestige and authority of their lady and her lord. In contrast to what will become the norm in later years, the word *dueña* in the *Cid* apparently has no relation to either the age or the marital status of these servants of category. [29] Also, in the poem we find attendant *dueñas* present at scenes of arrival and departure, where they only function to attest to the honor of their lord or lady. The figure of the *dueña* in the *Cid* underscores the familial nature of the poem and emphasizes the nobility of the principal characters.

III. *Libro del cauallero Zifar*

Dueñas and *doncellas* emerge as figures in certain traditional situations in chivalric literature. *Dueñas* and *doncellas* appear in the *Caballero Cifar* (c. 1300), the first work of Castilian literature that is chivalric in part. *Dueña* is the standard word to indicate 1) a noble lady and 2) married or widowed women as a group. The coupled term '*dueñas y doncellas*' refers to 1) married and unmarried women

---

[28] The Cid's wealth has grown to such an extent that he can give as a dowry to each of Doña Jimena's *dueñas* just double the amount he had given to the monastery of San Pedro de Cardeña for their support for an entire year at the time of his exile (I.15.252-254). It is evident that the Cid's honor grows in proportion to the honor he can bestow on the members of his household.

[29] See Menéndez Pidal, *Voc.*, 632. We do not know whether any of Doña Jimena's attendants are widows. In the romances, ladies are served by both "dueñas" and "doncellas" (*Cifar, Amadís,* etc.). The word "doncella" does not appear in the *Cid*. It seems that in the course of the thirteenth century the group of attendants was broken down more exactly into "dueñas," older and widowed, and "doncellas," younger and unmarried. Attendant "dueñas" and "doncellas" are mentioned in the *Siete Partidas* (see Ch. 1, note 1 above), and we find "duenna de alta guisa" and "donzella" in the *Primera Crónica General*, 773b15 (see Menéndez Pidal, *Voc.*, p. 337). I have not found 'doncella' used earlier than the thirteenth century. 'Doncela' appears in "Razón de Amor," l. 56, in *Libro de Alexandre*, strophe 1712 and 'doncellas' in Berceo, *Santa Oria*, strophe 45.

as a group and 2) widowed and unmarried (rarely married) ladies-in-waiting. *Doncella* appearing alone refers to youthful unmarried attendants.

The prime acceptation of *dueña* in the Cifar is noble lady. Grima, Cifar's wife, a perfect wife and mother, is always referred to as *dueña*. For instance, in the opening lines of Chapter I, we find:

> Cuenta la estoria que este cauallero auia vna dueña por muger que auia nonbre Grima e fue muy buena dueña e de buena vida e muy mandada a su marido e mantenedora e guardadora de la su casa ... [30]

In addition, the widowed noblewomen of the *Cifar* are consistently called *dueña*: among these are the Lady of Galapia (41) and the Lady of the Lake (227, 229). An example of *dueña* used to denote women in general may be found in the words of the Lady of the Lake to the Caballero Atrevido:

> E el cauallero dixo a la dueña: "Señora, que es esto por que esta gente non fabla?" "Non les fabledes," dixo [ella], "nin a ninguna dueña, maguer vos fablen, ca perderme-yedes porende" (228).

The ladies of the *Cifar* are attended and accompanied by *dueñas* and *doncellas*. While the status of the *dueñas* and *doncellas* who accompany the Lady of Galapia cannot be determined precisely, we may infer that they belong to the nobility. In the following scene the lady has fainted, believing that Cifar has been defeated in a battle in the defense of her town:

> E el duelo e las bozes de las dueñas e de las donzellas fueron muy grandes en el palaçio; ca todas las donzellas e dueñas que auia en la villa todas eran y con ella; ca las vnas tenian sus maridos en la hueste, e las otras sus hermanos e las otras sus parientes e sus padres e su fijos ... (65).

The focus is on the *dueñas* and *doncellas* as concerned wives, mothers and sisters.

---

[30] *El libro del Cauallero Zifar,* ed. Charles Philip Wagner (Ann Arbor, 1929), p. 9.

The focus is quite different in other appearances of *dueñas* and *doncellas*. The *dueñas* and *doncellas* who attend the Princess of Menton are honor attendants. They accompany her and are richly attired:

> La infante se vino luego con muchas dueñas e donzellas para ally do estaua el rey, mucho noblemente vestida ella e todas las otras que con ella venian (163).

The same is true of the *dueñas* and *doncellas* who attend the Infanta Seringa. She spends her time in their company. They appear to add to her prestige, for she seeks to honor and, probably, to impress Roboan by having a greater number of her ladies-in-waiting present for their second meeting:

> Deque ouo [Roboan] andado vna pieça por la çibdat fuese para casa de la infante. E quando a ella dixieron quel infante venia, plogole muy de coraçon e mando que acogiesen a el e a toda su conpaña. E la infanta estaua en el grant palaçio que el rey su padre mandara fazer, muy bien aconpañada de muchas dueñas e donzellas, mas de quantas fallo Roboan quando la vino ver en la mañana (390-391).

This same motive — prestige and authority — can be seen in the emphasis given them at the time of Seringa's arrival to marry Roboan:

> E la infante leuo consigo muchas dueñas e muchas donzellas, las mas fijas dalgo e mejor acostunbradas que en todo el regno auia, e fueron por todas çiento, vestidas de paño de oro e de seda ... El conde Amigo, que era ydo adelante, dixo al enperador de commo la infante Seringa era salida de su tierra e se venia para el, ... e ella que traya çient dueñas y donzellas muy fijas dalgo e muy bien vestidas (513).

In these passages *dueñas* and *doncellas* are mentioned for much the same reason that *dueñas* appear in the *Cid*: they indicate the social status of their ladies, and their presence is construed as a means of honoring and impressing an illustrious visitor.

Of more importance for our thesis are instances where *dueñas* and *doncellas* take part in scenes of arrival and departure, for we will have cause to examine Cervantes' parody of this situation in *Don Quijote*. *Dueñas* and *doncellas* are present at Grima's arrival at the Kingdom of Orbin:

> E el rey enbio luego a la reyna que saliese a la ribera
> con todas las otras dueñas e donzellas de la villa con las
> mayores alegrias que podiesen... E quando llegaron a la
> ribera, estaua y la reyna, e muchas donzellas faziendo sus
> danças. E desy salio el rey de la galea e tomo la dueña [Gri-
> ma] por la mano... (101).

Although *dueñas* and *doncellas* in this case are still mere background
figures, the "alegrías" and "danças" begin to suggest a stylization.
The scene foreshadows the pomp surrounding the arrival of an illustrious personage at a castle in later chivalric works. An example from
an earlier portion of the *Caballero Cifar* shows how the characteristic
features of the situation are still in a nascent stage. Cifar enters
Galapia accompanied by his entire family. They are greeted by *caballeros* and *dueñas*.

> E estos dos dias resçebieron mucha onrra e mucho plazer
> de la señora de la villa, e todos los caualleros e los omes
> buenos venian ver e a solazar con el Cauallero Zifar, e todas
> las dueñas con su muger, e fazianles sus presentes muy gran-
> damente (47).

The idea of a knight-errant's encountering adventures in the company
of his wife and children will seem strange if we wrongly assume *Cifar*
to be wholeheartedly in the chivalric spirit. [31] Castilian chivalric convention of later times has accustomed us to unmarried knights, who,
upon arrival at a castle, and after the traditional greeting by *dueñas*
and *doncellas* (not by *caballeros* and *dueñas*), are likely to engage in
exploits of both the "military" and the erotic kind. Such is not the
case here.

The story of Cifar's son, Roboan, of course, is closer to the
chivalric ideal than his father's. [32] The scenes of the "Hechos de
Roboan" where *dueñas* and *doncellas* appear foreshadow a later

---

[31] María Rosa Lida de Malkiel, *La idea de la fama en la Edad Media
castellana* (Buenos Aires, 1952), p. 260. James F. Burke, "A Critical and
Artistic study of the *Libro del Cavallero Cifar*," unpub. diss., University of
North Carolina (Chapel Hill, 1966), microfilm, points out the Cifar and his
sons are exponents of religious chivalry (p. 78) and that the largesse and
service to lady we expect to find in a romance of chivalry are lacking because
they would conflict with the overall purpose of the author (pp. 66-72).

[32] Wagner, "The Sources of *El Cavallero Cifar*," *Révue Hispanique* (1903),
X, p. 48.

development of certain topics. There are scenes of arrival and departure, with the typical participants, *caballeros, dueñas* and *doncellas,* in various stages of development. For instance, when Seringa greets the victorious Roboan, after his defeat of her enemies in battle, she is accompanied by her ladies-in-waiting:

> E quando el ynfante Roboan e la otra gente llegaron a la villa, la ynfanta salio con todas las dueñas e donzellas fuera de la çibdat... e esperaronlos alli, faziendo todos los de la çibdat muy grandes alegrias (409).

The ladies-in-waiting are mere figures, with but a slight coloring, as also in the scene of his departure from Pandulfa: "... e el infante se espedio della e de todas las otras dueñas e donzellas e de todos los otros omes buenos que y eran en el palaçio con la infante" (429).

A more detailed treatment is given to the scene of the knight's departure from his first wife, the Empress of the Insolas Dotadas:

> E la enperatris con sus dueñas e donzellas fincaron muy desconortadas e muy tristes, faziendo el mayor duelo del mundo, commo aquella que fincaua desfiuzada de lo nunca mas ver, en cuyo poder ella codiçiaua acabar sus dias (478).

The scene describing Roboan's return to the Empire of Trigrida approaches a complete stylization:

> Las nueuas llegaron a la çibdat, e quando la gente del infante lo oyeron fueron muy ledos, e salieron lo a resçebir... E grande fue el alegria que fue fecha en toda la tierra del enperador quando lo sopieron... E quando el infante entro con el enperador a la çibdat fueron fechas muy grandes alegrias, e non finco cauallero nin dueña nin donzella que alla non saliesen, deziendo a muy grandes bozes: "Bien sea venido el amigo leal del enperador" (482).

In addition to their appearance in such scenes, *dueñas* and *doncellas* are seen to be associated with the concept of knighthood and chivalry. They are invariably mentioned whenever a definition of a good knight or of a knight's duties is given. For example, we find *dueñas* and *doncellas* mentioned in a description of Roboan as a model medieval knight:

> ...Este era el mejor acostunbrado cauallero mançebo que ome en el mundo sopiese; ca era mucho apuesto en sy,

e de muy buen donario e de muy buena palabra e de buen
resçebir, e jugador de tablas e de axadres, e muy buen ca-
çador de toda aue mejor que otro ome ... partidor de su
auer muy francamente ally do conuenia, verdadero en su palabra, sabidor en los fechos, de dar buen consejo quando
gelo demandauan ... buen cauallero de sus armas con es-
fuerço e non con atreuimiento, onrrador de dueñas e de donzellas ... (386).

Roboan agrees to be the guest of Seringa at Pandulfa because he is a
good knight: "E el otorgogelo, ca nunca fue desmandado a dueña
nin a donzella de cosa quel dixiese, que fazedera fuese ..." (388). A
good knight is mindful of the wishes of women.

It remains for us to analyze the role played by *dueñas* and *doncellas* as individuals. They appear in situations that may be said to
preview the familiar *dueña*-in-distress, *doncella*-in-distress and, in a
lesser degree, intermediary *doncella* of the prose romances. The topic
of *dueña*-in-distress is incipient in the *Caballero Cifar*. It lacks as yet
the characteristics we associate with it from our knowledge of later
chivalric romances. For instance, although Cifar comes to the aid of
the *dueña* or *señora* of Galapia, who is at war with an enemy
(Chaps. 11-39), he is a reluctant guest, is anxious to be on his way,
and intervenes in the problems she faces only when specifically asked
to do so. Cifar ultimately ends further hostilities by arranging the
marriage of the lady to the son of her enemy.

Here we recognize the broad outline of the topic of *dueña*-in-
distress: a knight comes to the aid of a lady. However, in the *Cifar*
the knight stumbles upon the situation by chance. He is not sought
out by the lady because of his fame. It will be remembered that Cifar
has undertaken errantry only because unfortunate circumstance has
forced him to do so; he has no desire to find fame and fortune, nor
to prove himself as a knight. He is accompanied on this adventure by
his entire family — wife and sons. He is more concerned with provid-
ing for them than with finding adventures. A considerable advance
over this attitude is seen in the "Hechos de Roboan." Roboan sets
out from his land to gain knightly experience.[33] His very first encounter is with a Princess/*doncella*-in-distress:

---

[33] *Cifar*, pp. 252 and 253. Burke, however, interprets Roboan's journey
as a divine mission, the journey of Everyman (p. 48). On the simple level of
plot, nonetheless, it is true that Roboan wants to "vsar de caualleria."

Atanto andudieron que ouieron a llegar al regno de Pandulfa, donde era señora la infante Seringa ... E porque era muger, los reys sus vezinos de enderredor fazianle mucho mal e tomauanle su tierra, non catando mesura, la que todo ome deue catar contra las dueñas. E quando Roboan llego a la çibdat do la infante Seringa estaua, fue muy bien reçibido e luego fue a la infante a uer. E ella se leuanto a el e resçibiolo muy bien, faziendole grant onrra mas que a otros fazia quando venian a ella (387).

Roboan does not hesitate to offer his services when the Infanta hears that her lands have been invaded:

El infante, quando la oyo quexar, fue mouido a grant piedat, e pesole mucho con la soberuia quel fazian, e dixole asy: "Señora, enbiastes le nunca a dezir a este rey que vos este mal faze, que vos lo non feziese?" "Çertas," dixo la infante ... El infante Roboan se torno contra el conde e dixo asy: "Conde, mandat me dar vn escudero que vaya con vn mi cauallero que yo le dare, e que le muestre la carrera e la tierra, e yo enbiare a rogar aquel rey que por la su mesura, mientra yo aqui fuere en el vuestro regno, que so ome estraño, que por onrra de mi que vos non faga mal ninguno ... (392-393).

Dueñas and *doncellas* who are ladies-in-waiting have individual roles in the *Caballero Cifar*. When a *dueña* or a *donzella*, the latter in particular, steps out of the background in the prose romances, she plays a well-defined role in certain topics — intermediary *doncella*, for instance. In the *Cifar* these topics, as we have observed with other situations and scenes, are in a formative stage and only foreshadow what they will become in a romance like the *Amadís*. It is unusual for a *dueña* who is an honor attendant to step out of the background. The only example is the Dueña Gallarda episode. Although Gallarda's social rank is not mentioned in the text, her very presence among the ladies-in-waiting of royalty indicates nobility. She, a lovely widow, is one of Seringa's attendants. The *dueña*'s main characteristic is her daring speech and manner, a trait conspicuous from her first appearance. She is "vna dueña buida muy fermosa que auía nonbre la dueña Gallarda, commoquier que era atreuida en su fablar ..." (388). Her facile tongue and subsequent actions thus suggest a remote antecedent not for the *dueñas* of the prose romances but for the literary figure

of the late sixteenth and seventeenth centuries, the *dueña de servicio,*
who was ill-famed for her talkativeness. [34]

The core of the *dueña* Gallarda episode is her attempt to test the
patience and gallantry of Roboan, presumably to ascertain his worthi-
ness as a consort for her lady. In a series of comic interchanges between Roboan and Gallarda, she tries, by bringing the young knight
to the end of his patience through feigned stupidity, to provoke him
into a breach of gallantry (388-389). Their second encounter ends
badly for the forward *dueña,* for Roboan concludes that she is "alguna
dueña torpe" (394) and counters her sallies with a biting riposte that
puts an end to the trial. The *dueña* admits she has learned a lesson.

The scene in which Roboan lectures the repentant *dueña* on
seemingly behavior in men and women is clearly didactic. The author
reproaches the conduct of ladies-in-waiting indirectly:

> Certas non obraron poco las palabras de Roboan nin fue-
> ron de poca uirtud, ca esta fue despues la mejor guardada
> dueña en su palabra e la mas sosegada, e de mejor vida luego
> en aquel regno. Çertas, mester seria vn infante commo este
> en todo tienpo en las casas de las reynas y de las dueñas de
> grant lugar que casas tienen, que quando el se asentase con
> dueñas o con donzellas, que las sus palabras obrasen asy
> commo las de este infante, e fuesen de grant uirtud, para
> que sienpre fiziesen bien e guardasen su onrra (397).

Although Gallarda is not an intermediary for Seringa and Roboan, [35]
she does praise Roboan to her lady. The role of match-maker is filled
by the Infanta's uncle, who proposes marriage between the two for
reasons of state. While Gallarda is not a forerunner of the *dueñas* of
later chivalric romances, she displays some of the negative qualities
that will be developed much later in the *dueña de servicio.*

---

[34] Roger M. Walker, "Did Cervantes Know the *Cavallero Zifar?*," *BHS*
(1970), XLIX, pp. 120-127, speaks of striking similarities between Gallarda
and Doña Rodríguez (p. 125). The few similarities they share in common
arise from Gallarda's coincidentally having some negative qualities that would
later be ascribed to the *dueña de servicio* in the late sixteenth and seventeenth centuries. Doña Rodríguez is initially portrayed as a typical *dueña de
servicio.* Cervantes need not have been familiar with the *Cifar* and the *dueña*
Gallarda to give to his character defects ascribed to *dueñas* in his own time.

[35] There are no illicit love affairs in the religious and partially didactic
Cifar. For an analysis of love and marriage in the *Cifar* see Justina Ruiz de
Conde, "El Libro del cauallero Zifar," *El amor y el matrimonio secreto en
los libros de caballerías* (Madrid, 1948), Ch. 2, pp. 35-98.

Doncellas appearing alone, without accompanying *dueñas,* have a small but significant role in the *Caballero Cifar.* They are antecedents of the *doncella* as found in later romances, such as the *Amadís* or the *Sergas de Esplandián.* The literary treatment accorded them suggests some influence of the "matière de Bretagne." [36]

Although the Lady Nobleza is attended by both *dueñas* and *doncellas* (as in her sad parting from Roboan, 478), only *doncellas* have a role in guiding Roboan to their lady. Roboan arrives on a guideless boat to the rocky shores of the Insolas Dotadas, whose only entry is blocked by iron doors; these mysteriously open as he passes, closing behind him. At a second set of doors,

> ... fallo alli dos donzellas muy bien vestidas e muy apues-
> tas, en sendos palafrenes, e tenien vn palafren de las reindas
> muy bien ensellado e muy bien enfrenado, e desçendieron a
> el e besaronle las manos e fizieronle caualgar en aquel pa-
> lafren, e fueronse con el diziendole que su señora la enpera-
> driz lo enbiaua mucho saludar, e que lo salien a resçebir dos
> reys sus vasallos, con muy grand caualleria, e le besarien
> las manos e lo resçibirien por señor, e le ferien luego ome-
> naje todos los del inperio a la ora que llegase a la enpera-
> driz ... (457).

The *doncellas* have mysterious knowledge of Roboan's past, and explain the enchantment or spell over the island to him. One of the *doncellas* reads to Roboan from the "libro de la estoria de don Yuan," a book that wins much praise from the author (459). [37]

The Insolas Dotadas episode contrasts with the story of the Caballero Atrevido and the Señora de la Traición (226-242), in which

---

[36] Wagner, "Sources," 44-57. Although Wagner's assumptions on the influence of the "matière de Bretagne" in the *Cifar* have been questioned, we ought not to discount its importance altogether. Some *doncellas* even read to Roboan from "el libro de don Yuan" (p. 459).

[37] "E la donzella lleuaua el libro de la estoria de don Yuan e començo a leer en el. E la donzella leye muy bien e muy apuestamente e muy orde-nadamente, de guisa que entendie el infante muy bien todo lo que ella leye, e tomaua en ello muy gran plazer e gran solaz; ca çiertamente no ha ome que oya la estoria de don Yuan, que non resçiba ende muy grand plazer, por las palabras muy buenas que en el dizie. E todo ome que quisiere auer solaz e plazer, e auer buenas costunbres, deue leer el libro de don Yuan" (*Cifar,* 459).

the knight also foolishly loses his lady.[38] The role of the *doncellas* in this episode is to lead the knight and his lady to their marriage bed (231). In both cases, they enact to a certain degree the role of intermediary *doncella*.

Doncellas appear in the knighting of the Roboan in Trigrida. Firstly, every *doncella* in the town kisses him, as a token of good fortune. The next day the ceremony continues in church:

> E otro dia en la mañaña fue el enperador a la eglesia de Sant Iohan do velaua el infante, e oyo misa e sacolo a la puerta de la eglesia a vna grant pila de porfirio que estaua lleña de agua caliente, e fezieronle desnuyar so vnos paños muy nobles de oro, e metieronlo en la pila ... E andauan en derredor de la pila cantando todas las donzellas ... E trayan vna lança con vn pendon grande, e vna espada des-nuya, e vna camisa grande de sirgo e de alfojar, e vna gir-nalda de oro muy grande ... E la camisa vestiogela vna don-zella muy fermosa e muy fija dalgo, a quien copo la suerte que gela vestiese. E desque gela vestio, besolo e dixole: "Dios te vista de la su gracia!" e partiose dende, ca asy lo auian por costunbre ... (441).[39]

It is also *doncellas* who weave the magic banner that will protect Roboan from losing battles on the Insolas Dotadas.[40]

Dueñas and *doncellas* thus play an important role in the *Caballero Cifar*. They appear as attendants to noble ladies, and attest to their honor and dignity. In this capacity they are background figures. On rare occasion, either a *dueña* or a *doncella* may move to the fore in a novel situation. The only attendant *dueña* to do so is the Dueña Gallarda. Her calling attention to herself by her daring dialogue is

---

[38] In the Caballero Atrevido story the illusion is ascribed to the devil, and the experience viewed as negative. Here, however, the illusion is caused by enchantment of a benevolent nature, and the happiness it brings about is lost by the temptation of the devil.

[39] Burke identifies the social ritual as French rather than Hispanic (75-77). It is of interest to us, however, that in the *libros de caballerías* following the *Cifar doncellas* are often mentioned as present or participating in some way. They are part of the literary ceremony. See *Amadís*, I.4.44-45; *Palmerin*, I.11.22.

[40] These *doncellas* are seventy years old. They are seven holy ladies vowed to charity and good works. See *Cifar*, 499. In the *Cifar*, *dueña* and *doncella* generally indicate age and/or marital status, but, as is evident, the word may also be used in the sense of "virgin," regardless of age.

viewed negatively by the author. No *doncella* has as prominent a role as Gallarda. *Doncellas* do, however, have a significant role in the fabulous episodes, or where the chivalric material is focused, as in the dubbing of a knight. On the whole, the role of the *dueña* is more restricted than that of the *doncella*. In later chivalric romances the role of the attendant *dueña* will become even less important, and, conversely, the role of attendant *doncella* will become prominent.

There is a dichotomy in the *Caballero Cifar* in the roles of *dueñas* and *doncellas*. The *dueña* — both lady and lady-in-waiting — generally appears as grave and serious, with the *doncellas* enjoying a more ethereal role. Since this divergence is even more evident in *Amadís de Gaula*, it would be well to seek an explanation for this difference before proceeding.

We have seen the *dueña* in the *Cid* as part of the household of a nobleman, where she evidences honor and prestige by her mere presence. The *dueña* emerges in the first work of Spanish literature as a reflection of peninsular feudal society in which the Cid and his wife move. The *Cid*, contrasted with the *Chanson de Roland*, for instance, is basically a familial epic, and the figure of the *dueña* is drawn from surrounding society. The same would seem to be true of the *Cifar*. The Dueña of Galapia is concerned with maintaining her estate and her authority. Dueña Gallarda is also a character drawn from reality; at least, she is made an example of for the benefit of real *dueñas*. The ideal is that a *dueña* should be serious and discreet, not lively and talkative. Cifar's wife, Grima, is an exemplary wife and mother. The tradition of love-service is not characteristically associated with the *dueñas* of the Castilian prose romances. Love for these *dueñas* was maternal, not romantic. When *doncellas* appear in early Medieval Castilian works, however, they are young girls, virgins. [41] The figure of the "wandering damsel," so typical of Arthurian romance, is not found in any extant work of Castilian literature through the early fourteenth century. This romantic figure does not appear in the *Cifar*, and because of the religious and allegorical intent of its author, we would not expect it. From the "wandering damsel" is drawn the familiar *doncella*-in-distress. The topic is not found in Castile, but in Arthurian legend filtering across the Pyrenees.

---

[41] Boggs, 198 refers us to *Conde Lucanor, Libro de Buen Amor* and *Santa Oria* for this acceptation. Another example from Berceo, *Santa Oria* may be seen on page 18 of this chapter.

There is no damsel comparable to Lunete, of Chrétien's *Yvain*, for example, in extant works before the *Amadis* in Castile. Chrétien gives a summary of her role:

> La dameisele ot non Lunete
> e fu une avenanz brunete,
> molt sage, et veziee, et cointe.
> A mon seignor Gauvain s'acointe
> qui molt la prise, et qui molt l'ainme,
> et por ce s'amie la clainme,
> qu'ele avoit de mort garanti
> son conpaignon et son ami;
> si li offre molt son servise.
> Et ele li conte de devise
> a con grant poinne ele conquist
> sa dame, tant que ele prist
> mon seignor Yvain a mari,
> et comant ele le gari
> des mains a cez qui le queroient;
> entre'ax ert, et si nel veoient. [42]

Lunete is a free agent, to a certain extent, wandering far with messages from her lady (31, 1005). She functions as intermediary and messenger. She is described as "fair and charming" (30, 974). Lunete provides an example of a damsel who appears in several Arthurian topics: intermediary damsel (49-64, 1552-2052), messenger damsel (31, 1005) and damsel-in-distress (108-113, 3557-3717), being condemned to death for her part in the marriage between Yvain and her lady.

Many wandering damsels appear in Chrétien's *Le Chevalier de la Charrete*. They, too, are intelligent and wise, and have a certain degree of autonomy, even when their journeys are undertaken at the bidding of the lady they serve. The damsel who points out to Gawain and the Knight of the Cart the way to Guinevere does not appear to serve any mistress, and is described as responding "intelligently" (p. 19, l. 612). She informs the knights of the obstacles they will meet. A *damoisele*, a lady, met on the road offers Lancelot shelter on the condition he sleep with her. She too is "fair and charming" (29, 934). The damsel puts the knight through a series of tests (pp. 29-40), and

---

[42] *Les romans de Chrétien de Troyes*, v. 4, *Le Chevalier au Lion*, ed. Mario Roques (Paris, 1967), p. 74, l. 2417-2432.

accompanies him for a time on the road. This damsel appears to serve otherworld forces. Damsels in the service of otherworld forces, having mysterious knowledge of events or connected with mysterious tests of knights, such as the damsel in question, are quite frequent in Arthurian romance. A wise and clever damsel is sent by Guinevere to Lancelot to bid him do his worst (and his best) at a tournament (pp. 172, 178). Damsels in the *Chevalier de la Charrete* are seen in the same roles — wandering damsel, messenger damsel, intermediary damsel — as in *Yvain*.

Clearly, these damsels are idealized and romanticized beings, and we might well ask ourselves why this is so. Loomis traces some of the damsels of Arthurian romance to figures of Celtic mythology. [43] He traces Grail damsels through Blathat to flower maidens or vegetation goddesses. Gawain's loves, Lunete among them, as Chrétien indicates (p. 74, ll. 2411-2412), can also be traced to mythological figures, such as moon goddesses (301). Likewise, Morgan le Fay (originally the Lady of the Lake) may find her origins in the Gallo-Roman goddess Matrona, a figure Loomis links to water (193). The damsels of the French romances were initially mythological personifications endowed with special qualities that set them apart from the ordinary damsels of society.

We can now suggest that *dueñas* and *doncellas*, coupled as early as the *Caballero Cifar*, where their functions or roles already differed when treated individually, may be traced to two different branches of literature. The serious and grave *dueñas*, reflecting the customs and concerns of society, are found in the Castilian epic, where they personified a social ideal. *Doncellas* may be traced through Arthurian romance to mythological figures. Evidence of this development, consistent with distant origin in two distinct genres, may be seen in *Amadís de Gaula*.

IV. *Amadís de Gaula*

The *Amadís de Gaula*, revised by Garci Rodríguez de Montalvo and published in 1508, but dating, in a more primitive form, from the fourteenth century, shows a marked advancement over the *Caballero Cifar* in the development of the roles of *dueñas* and *doncellas*.

---

[43] Roger Sherman Loomis, *Celtic Myth and Arthurian Romance* (New York, 1927), pp. 281-282. See also p. 287 and p. 193.

Dueña, of course, is still the standard term meaning "woman," married, widowed or middle aged. In this acceptation *dueña* usually denotes a noblewoman. The widow Grasinda, for instance, is a noblewoman. She first appears in the *Amadís* as a "dueña vestida de muy ricos paños," accompanied by a large entourage of *caballeros, dueñas* and *doncellas.* [44] Even a *dueña* as noble as Grasinda can pass into the service of royalty, as when she becomes one of Oriana's honor attendants (*dueñas*). The queens are also called *dueña.* Elisena's mother, the Queen, is referred to as "vna noble dueña" (I.11), and Elisena herself is also a "dueña" (II.3.37). The division between literary mode and social usage and reality at the beginning of the sixteenth century is apparent here. "Dueña" in this sense is medieval usage, and had become primarily literary by 1508.

Dueñas (ladies, not ladies-in-waiting) have an important role in the romance. The topic of *dueña*-in-distress is developed to a considerable extent in Book IV of the *Amadís.* Ladies seek the aid of a knight in a time of need. The three *dueñas* who have need of aid in Book IV are women of rank, although they do not seem to be members of the highest nobility. The topic is more fully developed than in the *Caballero Cifar.* In the *Cifar,* and elsewhere in the *Amadís,* a knight may come across a distressed *dueña* by chance; he is not deliberately sought out by the lady because of his fame and reputation. Cifar comes upon the besieged Lady of Galapia by chance (40-43), and Galaor also comes upon the *doncella* who leads to his avenging the death of Antebón for his widow, a *dueña,* by chance. In Book IV, a lady searches for a knight because she is aware of his reputation.

The *dueña*-in-distress as she appears in the chivalric romances, and particularly in *Amadís de Gaula,* is of special interest, for two related episodes of *Don Quijote,* Part II are based on it. The "Dueña Dolorida" episode is a parody of the topic. Doña Rodríguez, a mere *dueña de servicio,* becomes the second "*dueña*-in-distress" of 1615. Her only knowledge of the common chivalric topic, which she does not recognize as literary, comes from the Trifaldi episode. A given set

---

[44] *Amadís de Gaula,* ed. Edwin B. Place, 4 vols. (Madrid, 1959-1971), III.72.783. Grasinda is a beautiful, rich noblewoman. She falls in love with Amadís, but resigned to her hopeless situation, she then aids him in every way. She accompanies him and becomes one of Oriana's ladies-in-waiting, presumably out of respect for Amadís. At this point, the author loses interest in her as a character.

of circumstances leads her to confuse her identity with the *dueñas* we will describe below.

Darioleta, Elisena's former *doncella,* is the first of the three *dueñas-in-distress* of Book IV. It is clear in her reunion with Amadís on the Insola Firme that, as a *dueña,* she is not an attendant, but rather a lady, wife of the governor of Brittany. She seeks Amadís out so that he may rescue her husband and daughter from the giant Balán, who has already slain her only son. The *dueña's* actions give evidence of her great anxiety and sorrow:

> ...Luego conoçió que era Amadís, y començo a romper sus tocas y vestiduras faziendo muy gran duelo y diziendo:
> —¡O señor Amadís de Gaula!, accorred a esta triste sin ventura por lo que deuéys a cauallería... pues que para acorrer y remediar los atribulados y corridos en este mundo naçistes en tanta amargura como sobre mí es venida.
> Amadís huuo muy gran duelo de la dueña... Y llegóse a ella, y quitándole las manos de los cauellos, que la mayor parte dellos era blanca, le preguntó qué cosa era aquella por que assí lloraua y tan duramente sus cabellos messaua; que ge lo dixesse luego y que no dexaría de poner su vida al punto de la muerte porque su gran pérdida reparada fuesse.
> La dueña, quando esto le oyó, hincóse delante dél de ynojos, quísole besar las manos, mas él no ge los quiso dar... (IV.127.1246).

We note that Darioleta cries, tears at her clothing and hair; she invokes the knight's aid in the name of chivalry; she kneels before him to express her gratitude for his undertaking the cause.

The adventure in itself consists in Amadís' battle with the giant Balán, and Balán's son Bravor (IV.128.1259-1263). Its successful conclusion is highlighted by Amadís' intervention as match-maker between the daughter and Bravor. He proposes their marriage, an idea which meets with general approval. The marriage is celebrated, and we are told that it will lead to an illustrious line of descendents (IV.129.1273).

The format of the other two cases of distressed ladies seeking justice through the intervention of knights in their troubles is quite similar. The "dueña de Noruega" has recourse to Agrajes, but Gandalín undertakes the adventure. The *dueña* is dressed in mourning, and casts herself at Agraje's feet.

> ...vn día entró por la tienda de Agrajes vna dueña del
> reyno de Nuruega, cubierta toda de negro, que se echó a
> los pies de Agrajes demandándole muy afincadamente que
> la quisiesse socorrer en vna tribulación en que estaua. Agra-
> jes la fizo leuantar y la sentó cabe sí, y demandóla que le
> dixiese qué cuyta era la suya, que él le daría remedia si con
> justa causa fazerse pudiese... (IV.130.1298).

Her *cuita* consists in having had her daughter abducted by a knight
the mother considers unworthy for the girl. This episode, like the
first, ends in marriage because of the intervention of Amadís, who
takes pity on the lovelorn knight. The girl is touched by her knight's
devotion, and Gandalín, on Amadís' instructions, intervenes with the
dueña so that the marriage may take place (1302).

A detail distantly recalling the Doña Rodríguez episode is that
the *dueña* must have recourse to Agrajes because her own King cannot
do justice in the case. It will be recalled that Doña Rodríguez appeals
to Don Quijote because the Duke did not respond to her plea for
justice. Here the reference is brief:

> Agrajes le dixo: "Dueña, ¿cómo el rey vuestro señor no
> os faze justicia?" "Señor" —dixo ella—, "el rey es ya muy
> viejo y doliente, de forma que ni a sí ni a otro puede gouer-
> nar" (IV.130.1299).

The last *dueña*-in-distress is Arcalaus' wife. Like the Dueña de
Noruega, she is dressed in black. She kneels before Amadís, appealing
to his adherence to the chivalric code:

> ...La dueña supo... cómo aquél era Amadís, y aten-
> diólo... Y como lo vió venir, fue contra él llorando, y fin-
> có los ynojos en tierra y díxole:
> —Mi señor Amadís, ¿no soys vos aquel cauallero que a
> los atribulados y mezquinos socorre, en especial a las dueñas
> y donzellas? Ciertamente si assí no fuesse, no sería vuestra
> gran fama por todas partes del mundo con tanta prez diuul-
> gada. Pues yo, como una de las más tristes y sin ventura, os
> demando misericordia y piedad.
> Entonces le trauó por la falda de la loriga con las manos
> ambas tan fuerte que solo vn passo no lo dexaua andar.
> Amadís la quiso leuantar, mas no pudo; y díxole:
> —Buena amiga, dezidme quién soys y para qué queréys
> mi acorro, que según la gran tristeza vuestra, ahunque a
> todas las otras dueñas fallesciesse, por vos sola pornía mi

persona a todo peligro y afruenta que me venir pudiesse
(IV.130.1304-1305).

The *dueña*'s woes are caused by the imprisonment of her husband.
By failing to identify herself, however, she deceives Amadís. The
knight, having promised to aid her without full knowledge of the
situation, is bound by the chivalric code to free, against his will, the
enchanter he himself had imprisoned. However, the *dueña*, described
as "pious," is presented as a positive figure.

In these cases we have been dealing solely with *dueñas* who are
ladies of rank. The *dueña de honor*, of course, forms part of the
group of ladies-in-waiting who attend the principal ladies of the
romance. Since the fact that *dueñas* and *doncellas* indicate the status
and prestige of the ladies they attend has been sufficiently explored
above, I do not think it is necessary to dwell on it here. Such was the
case in the *Cid* and in the *Cifar*; so it is in the *Amadís*. Elisena
(I.3.36), Brisena (III.66.699) and Grasinda (III.72.75) are often seen
in the company of their waiting ladies. In part, Dinarada, the sham
"doncella muda," is recognized as wealthy because of the "dueñas
y donzellas" who regard her as "señora" (III.69.737). Amadís impres-
ses Brisena by the size and quality of his entourage, among whom,
beside the noble knights, there are "dueñas y donzellas de tan alta
guisa" (IV.123.1217). *Dueñas* and *doncellas* in this frame of reference
do not have developed roles. They do take part as figures in the
traditional scenes of arrival and departure. It is rare for any of these
attendants to step forward from the group to undertake significant
action. However, individual *doncellas* enjoy a more prominent role
in the *Amadís* than they did in the *Cifar*. The role of "dueña de
honor," in contrast, is of little importance in the *Amadís*.

A nameless *dueña*, accompanied by two *doncellas*, is sent by her
lady, Celinda, on an important mission to Lisuarte. She requests that
Lisuarte knight the youth Norandel, later disclosing secretly to the
king the paternity of the young man (III.66.691-692; 694-695). It
might be well to point out the *dueña*'s characteristics, despite her
brief role. The author indicates her age, noting "no era muy moça."
She is associated, albeit indirectly, with an illicit love affair by virtue
of bringing the son born of that union to his father. However, she is
a positive character, and is treated with respect. Another *dueña* has a
most brief and colorless role in the romance. One of Oriana's *dueñas*

guards a door leading to the garden where her lady is resting. She announces the arrival of Amadís' dwarf (IV.117.1170). The author's lack of interest in attendant *dueñas* can be observed through his treatment of the *dueña* Grasinda. She is a figure of some importance and prominence as a *dueña* of estate, protectress of Amadís, but her role is radically diminished when she passes into Oriana's service, being mentioned on only one or two occasions.

It is the *doncellas* who enjoy a more prominent position in the book, functioning as intermediaries and messengers for the knights and ladies. Darioleta, who is termed "discreta" and "sesuda" (23), recalling the clever and prudent damsels of Arthurian romance, is confidante to Elisena's love for Perión. She brings Elisena to the knight's chamber at night, first having extracted from him a promise of marriage (I.14-15). She controls the situation, planning the manner of the meeting. She is also in charge of matters during Amadís' birth, for Darioleta devises the plan to save her lady's public honor and life, and saves Amadís' life too (I.1.22-24). The Doncella de Dinamarca, an attendant *doncella,* is the confidante of Oriana, serving as constant messenger between Oriana and Amadís. She undertakes long journeys for her lady. It is she who sets out to search for Amadís during his penitence on the Peña Pobre (II.52.423).

There are several *doncellas,* either ladies of rank themselves or in the service of ladies, who wander on the roads, afoot or on palfreys. For example, Galaor meets two wandering *doncellas,* travelling separately, at a cross road. One of the *doncellas* is on her way to witness singular combat between a knight and the giant of the Peña de Galtares. This *doncella*'s role is merely to report what she sees to her lady. The second damsel, without naming her mission, decides to accompany Galaor and the first damsel. We later learn she was travelling to see her brother at Lisuarte's court (I.12.101). Upon Galaor's successful battle with the giant (for he has decided to undertake this adventure himself), the first *doncella* leads Galaor to an erotic and secret adventure (I.12.105). Her lady, Aldeva, favors Galaor with her love simply because he is the best knight she knows. Galaor later encounters another *doncella* who leads him to her knight so that they might do battle (I.21.188-190). Another damsel on a palfrey, of the house of Antebón, leads this same knight to the castle of her lady, so that he might avenge Antebón's death, and an injustice against the house. Two other *doncellas* lead him to the castle where the daughter of Antebón is being held captive (215-223). It is not surprising that it is Galaor who most frequently engages in adventures with damsels. Amadís does also on occasion, but the episodes and scenes are never erotic in nature, for his loyalty to Oriana precludes such a turn of events. Galaor has no such loyalties.

Even when these damsels are in the service of a lady they enjoy freedom of movement and autonomy and are able to exercise discretion. They are in the line of the damsels of Arthurian romance. They often lead the knight to adventures, both chivalric and romantic (that is, erotic). The *dueña* is never seen to function in the same way as these wandering *doncellas*. Indeed, while Aldeva's *doncella* wanders about and brings Galaor to her lady, the other "dueñas y doncellas" quietly sleep (105). Although Darioleta is not a "wandering" *doncella,* for she does not leave the company of her lady, her evolution in the *Amadís* from *doncella* to *dueña* demonstrates the distinct roles of the two.

As a *doncella* in Book I she is wise and discreet. Idealized by the author, Darioleta is a prominent figure whose actions are decisive and important because of her role as confidante and intermediary. We can actually say that without Darioleta there would have been no Amadís. She is in the line of descent of a Lunete, as are many of the wandering *doncellas* of the *Amadís*. [45] As a *dueña* in Book IV, she reminds us of a Doña Jimena, or of a Grima. She is seen only as a concerned wife and mother. Now older and afflicted, her role contrasts with her former one. She is the helpless victim of injustice. The literary precedents of Darioleta as *doncella* are to be sought in Arthurian romance, and as *dueña* in medieval Castilian works.

Urganda la Desconocida, the wise enchantress, is also both *dueña* and *doncella,* changing her physical appearance at will. She consistently appears as a *doncella,* with one exception, in Book I. The author does not present a detailed description, but is interested in details of age and youth. The first description of her in Book I is rather vague:

> . . . [El rey Perión] saliendo al palacio falló vna donzella más garnida de atauíos que fermosa, y díxole: —Sábete, rey Perión que quando tu pérdida cobrares, perderá el señorío de Yrlanda su flor (I.2.28).

---

[45] Among these are Dinamarca, and in particular, Aldeva's *doncella,* who, like Lunete, suffers imprisonment for her intervention.

Another early appearance is her form change before the eyes of a startled Gandules, where age — indicating the change from *doncella* to *dueña* — is emphasized:

> Y sabe que mi nombre es Urganda la Desconocida; agora me cata bien y conósceme si pudieres.
>
> Y él que [Gandules] la vio donzella de primero, que a su parecer no passaua de diez y ocho años, viola tan vieja y tan lassa que se marauilló como en el palafren se podía tener; y començose a santiguar de aquella marauilla (I.2.30).

She is also called *doncella* in I.3.36, I.5.49, I.11.94 and II.59.500-501. After this point she always appears a dueña (lady). In the guise of *doncella* she personally brings prognostications to kings (Lisuarte, Perión), reveals paternities, and guides the fate of Amadís and Galaor. She appears suddenly to the characters on the by-ways and roads. We shall see that in her later appearances as a *dueña*, she comes to the characters in a more formalized and grave manner.

The transformation to *dueña* occurs in II.59.501-502. It is logical to assume that Urganda is both the *dueña* who ministers to Cildadán's wounds and the *doncella* who attends to Galaor's. [46] Urganda, in this

---

[46] The author identifies the *doncella* as Urganda, but at no time does he tell us who the *dueña* is. The two wounded knights are carried by twelve damsels to a mysterious tower where they are alternately terrified and cared for, as part of the cure. A *doncella*, who is amused at Galaor's mention of Urganda, gives him healing ointments. At this point we read:

> 1 [El rey Cildadán] vio abrir una puerta de piedra que en la torre enxerida era, tan junta que no paresçía sino la misma pared, y vio entrar por ella una dueña de media edad y dos caualleros armados. Y llegaron al lecho donde él estaua, mas no le saludaron, y él a ellos sí, hablándoles con buen semblante... La dueña le quitó el cobertor que sobre sí tenía, y catándole las llagas, le puso en ellas melezinas y diole de comer. Y tornaronse por donde vinieron sin palabra le dezir (II.59.502).

No more is said about the *dueña*. Now a *doncella* appears in Galaor's room, and she identifies herself as Sabiencia Sobresabiencia (that is, Urganda):

> 2 [Galaor] quando pensando en aquello y vieniendole a la memoria la fermosa espada que Urganda, al tiempo que su hermano le fizo cauallero, le dio, suspechó que ésta podría ser; pero dudaua en ello, porque en aquella sazon la vio muy vieja, y agora moça; por esto no la conocio (II.59.502).

Despite the author's not naming the *dueña*, I believe we may safely identify her as Urganda. Since she heals Galaor in person, she most probably would do the same for Cildadán. More importantly, at no time in the four books of the *Amadís* is Urganda seen to have *dueñas* in her service. Her messen-

episode, comes close to functioning as a go-between. She sends her two young nieces to the knights, with the result that the two girls conceive and give birth:

> ... Mandó a dos sobrinas suyas, muy fermosas donzellas, fijas del rey Falangrís ... que los sirviessen y visitassen y acabassen de sanar. La vna dellas Julianda se llamaua, la otra Solisa; en la qual visitación se dio causa a que dellos fuessen preñadas de dos fijos: el de Don Galaor Talanque llamado, el del rey Cildadán Maneli el Mesurado, los quales muy valientes y esforçados caualleros salieron, assi como adelante se dirá (II.59.503).

Whether Urganda intended to act as a go-between is conjectural, as is the question of how much of the episode is Montalvo's fabrication. The involved and complicated explanation of the affair given by Urganda at the close of Book IV carries Montalvo's stamp. She claims responsibility as the prime mover of the affair. She herself could not bear children ("pues que en mi propia persona ninguna generación engendrarse puede"), so she has raised the two children. The virtue of the young men will bring divine pardon to "aquellos que contra el mandamiento de la santa yglesia los engendraron, y a mí que lo causé" (IV.126.1236).

In subsequent appearances in the *Amadís* Urganda is an imposing *dueña*. She arrives at Lisuarte's court in a candle-lit boat decked with flowers. She is accompanied by ten damsels who are richly dressed (II.60.512). Her appearance at court with Talanque and Maneli is even more impressive, for she comes on the fearsome dragon-boat (IV.12.1220-1221). She appears again in the "fusta de la Gran Serpiente" at the book's close, and is greatly honored (IV.133.1333-1334). Her advice is heeded by all.

Urganda is a character inspired in Arthurian romance; she reminds us of a Morgan le Fay. She cannot be considered a prototype for

---

gers and attendants are always *doncellas* (cf. II.57.482; II.58.495; II.60.512 and III.68.724). The form-changing Urganda is most likely doing that in these two passages.

I would like to point out here, at the risk of introducing further complications, a lapse of memory on the author's part in the second quotation above. Galaor has never seen Urganda as old. In the incident Galaor remembers, she is called "donzella." He himself addressed her then as "donzella" (I.11.94). Urganda's only appearance as an old woman was the transformation of I.2.30.

dueñas of later books of chivalry in that she is the equal of kings and emperors, and is indeed superior to them by virtue of her magical powers. She has more in common with Merlin than she does with a Viuda Reposada, for instance.

V. *Sergas de Esplandián*

The *Sergas de Esplandián* (1511) does not show any divergency from the *Amadís de Gaula* in the treatment of *dueñas* and *doncellas*. Needless to say, the great ladies are all attended by *dueñas* and *doncellas,* who maintain their customary background role. [47] The role of the *doncella* Carmela is outstanding. She presents an example of a *doncella* who attends a knight rather than a lady. Thus, Esplandián's faithful *doncella* carries messages from her lord Esplandián to Leonorina (cf. 60.464). She devises the ingenious plan to secret Esplandián in Leonorina's room by night (93.490). She demonstrates initiative, and has freedom of mobility. She gains considerable standing among kings because of her great discretion (426). The *doncella* Queen Menoresa guards over her lady Leonorina's chastity and honor during the nocturnal visit of Esplandián (96.493-494). [48]

The *dueñas* are of but minor interest. The *dueña* Arcabona (Queen and enchantress), sister of Arcalaus, first enchants Lisuarte, but is foiled by Esplandián. She goes to Lisuarte, now freed, so that he might save her son's life, although the health of the son is certainly not in Lisuarte's hands. Her actions are those of a concerned mother:

> Acabada la cena, vínose la dueña madre del Gigante donde el Rey estaba; y él como la vió, levantóse á ella y hízola asentar cabe sí, y preguntóle cómo quedaba su hijo. Ella respondió ... Pero á lo que yo, Rey, vengo á ti, no es á te demandar perdon del mal y daño que te hice, porque muy mas contenta seria que en mí ejecutases la pena que merezco, la cual será darme la muerte, por donde á mis grandes angustias y dolores se dará fin. Y pues que nunca hasta agor á dueña ni á doncella en cosa que demandasen les fallecistes, no me fallezcas á mí, habiéndolo tanto menester ... (9.417).

[47] Garci Rodríguez de Montalvo, *Las Sergas del muy esforzado Caballero Esplandian,* ed. Pascual de Gayangos, *BAE,* vol. 40 (Madrid, 1874). See 5.410.411; 26.432; 29.435; 40.454; 80.480; 120.520; 127.526.

[48] In this case, a queen serves as *doncella* to an even nobler *infanta,* daughter of the Emperor of Constantinople.

Arcabona is a variation of the *dueña cuitada* or *menesterosa*. She comes to Lisuarte to seek his aid, and implores him in the name of his duties as a knight to women. However, this *dueña*, contrary to the rule, is seen in a most negative light. After her son's death, she seeks vengeance, but the attempt ends in her own death.

VI. *Demanda del Sancto Grial*

The *Demanda del Sancto Grial* (1515) does not present any significant divergencies with respect to the pattern outlined in the preceding pages. It does, however, have an episode of interest in Chapters 91-96. A *dueña* appears as a figure in the topic of the nocturnal visit of a damsel to a knight's chambers. A *dueña*, governess to King Bricos' daughter, unsuccessfully tries to prevent the damsel from going to Galaz' chambers. Described as a "dueña de gran guisa," [49] she tries to discharge her duty well. She is the confidante of the princess, but does not approve of her ward's sentiments. Convinced that she has dissuaded the damsel from folly, she is deceived:

> "Señora, sabed que yo amo vno de los caualleros aqui estan atan de coraçon, que si lo no ouiesse a mi voluntad, nunca jamas auria bien..." e quando el ama esto oyo, ouo muy gran pesar... entonce dixo el ama a la donzella: "¡Ay cosa mezquina e loca! ¿y que es esto que oyo? O has el seso perdido, o eres encantada, ca tu eres dueña de gran guisa, y eres tan hermosa, e tu coraçon has metido en vn cauallero estraño que no sabes quien es, e oy vino e mañana se va, e por le dar su padre toda su tierra morira ante que fincar aqui; e tu moriras por lo que dizes"... E quando la donzella esto oyo, fue muy mal espantada... "Agora me dezid, dixo el ama, ¿pareceos buen consejo el que vos yo dixe, que no es bueno poner vuestro coraçon en aquel cauallero?" "Si, dixo ella, porque no puedo fazer al, que no pueden fazer todos de su coraçon lo que quieren;" "¡Como! dixo la dueña, ¡no lo fagades si escarnida no queredes ser!"... Luego dixo la donzella a su ama por se encobrir, mas otra cosa tenia en su coraçon... (92, 93.196-197).

Galaz, a Grail knight vowed to chastity, turns down the girl, and strongly reproaches her conduct. The girl commits suicide with Galaz' own sword. The episode ends in a battle.

---

[49] *Demanda del Sancto Grial...*, *Libros de caballerías*, v. 1, ed. Adolfo Bonilla y San Martín, *NBAE*, vol. 6 (Madrid, 1907), Chap. 91, p. 196.

This is the only *dueña* I know of among the attendants of the Castilian romances who is seen to be in charge of a young girl, and is directly associated with an illicit affair in some way. The role of intermediary and confidante is given always to a *doncella*. In this case, however, the *dueña*'s actions are to be viewed in a positive light, and there is no transposition of the role of *doncella* to a *dueña*. The *dueña* is not an intermediary. To the contrary, she tries to prevent an illicit affair.

VII. *Palmerín de Inglaterra*

We will close this investigation of *dueñas* and *doncellas* in the Castilian prose romances with a study of their appearances in *Palmerín de Inglaterra* (1547), an example of the Renaissance prose romances. There is no significant change in their roles or appearances in comparison to the earlier or medieval romances. They are found in situations typical of romances we have studied. We will classify these appearances and typical situations according to relative importance — figure, topic — in this last text, so that when we come to the same situations in *Don Quijote*, Part II, we can clearly identify the situations Cervantes alludes to.

Dueñas and *doncellas,* so coupled as ladies-in-waiting, are characteristically mere figures in certain typical situations. They are simply mentioned as being present at scenes of arrival. For instance, they are present with their lady to receive Don Duardos at a castle:

> ... [Don Duardos] entró en el patio, y de ahí subió a una sala, donde fue recebido de una dueña, que en su presencia representaba ser persona de merecimiento, tiniendo tal presencia y auctoridad, que obligaba á todo hombre tratalla con mayor acatamiento de lo que sus obras merecían. Estaba acompañada de algunas dueñas y doncellas, y con ellas le vino á recebir con tan gran placer, como le hacía tener tenello en su poder. [50]

While the treatment given *dueñas* and *doncellas* here does not differ from what may be found in earlier romances, the reference to the *dueña* (lady) does give us some pause. She is described as being

---

[50] *Libro del muy esforzado Caballero Palmerín de Inglaterra, Libros de caballerías,* v. 2, ed. A. Bonilla y San Martín (Madrid, 1908), I.1.6.

"persona de merecimiento," and as having "tal presencia y auctoridad." The words, of course, are used to contrast her noble outward appearance with her true character. However, before 1547 no author of romances would have expressed the qualities inherent in *dueñas* in such a manner, for a *dueña*, by definition, was a noble lady of estate and authority. The actions of a given *dueña* could either conform to the norm (Grasinda) or differ from it (Arcabona). At this later date, it would seem that the author felt the necessity to clarify in some way what a *dueña* was. The acceptation of dueña=lady was already isolated in the prose romances in the sixteenth century.

Dueñas and *doncellas* accompany their ladies at jousts or singular combat:

> 1. Acabado de comer, el emperador se fue al cadahalso donde había de ver los torneos, acompañado de algunos señores á quien las edades antiguas detenían en Costantinopla... La emperatriz y Gridonia, con sus dueñas y doncellas, se pusieron en otro que para ellas estaba señalado... (I.11.22).

> 2. El gigante Almaurol, espantado de la braveza de aquella batalla, como aquel que nunca viera otra tal, llevando las nuevas della a Miraguarda, no tardó mucho que á una ventana se puso un paño de seda bordado de trozos de oro para de allí la mirar acompañada de sus dueñas y doncellas... (I.60.107).

These *dueñas* and *doncellas* are not described, and take no part in the action of the story. As figures, they arouse no interest in either the author or the reader. They are ornamental figures who stylize a traditional background. Rarely is an elaboration of what their duties entail undertaken. One brief exception is a reference to Leonarda's attendants:

> ...Dice la historia que como ya estuviesse en este tiempo determinada la partida de la princesa Leonarda para la corte del emperador Palmerín, quiso la reina Carmelia su agüela envialla bien acompañada, assí de dueñas para su autoridad como de doncellas para su servicio, y algunos señores del reino para honralla en su viaje... (II.10.210).

It is significant that the author has chosen to make even so brief a reference ("dueñas para su autoridad... doncellas para su servicio") to the functions of the *dueñas* and *doncellas*. In similar scenes in the *Cid*, the *Caballero Cifar*, or in the *Amadís*, the emphasis was on the high category of the *dueñas* and *doncellas* rather than on their duties, which were never mentioned. It would seem that the author of a mid-sixteenth-century prose romance could interpret the roles of *dueñas* and *doncellas* in a manner more suited to the contemporary servants of society than to the chivalresque figures he is describing.

The coupling also appears in topics, such as the frequently cited formulae of the romances that refer to the duties of knights. It will be remembered that the coupling in this context refers to women in general, and not specifically to ladies-in-waiting. Palmerín is described as a typical knight who aids *dueñas* and *doncellas*:

> ... Tornará el auctor á dar cuenta del caballero de la Fortuna; que después que se partió de Pompides, anduvo por tierras estrañas socorriendo *dueñas* y *doncellas*, deshaciendo agravios á muchos, haciendo cosas tan señaladas en armas con que su fama estendía por el mundo ... (I.24.41).

He is later asked to aid Colambrar by her *dueña*, who invokes his aid in the name of his reputation:

> "Ruégoos, señor caballero, que pues para vencer vuestros enemigos tenéis esfuerzo sobrado, que para socorrer las dueñas y doncellas no os falte misericordia y piedad; este pueblo trabaja por matar á Colambrar mi señora ..." (II.17.233).

The familiar topics of *dueña*-in-distress and *doncella*-in-distress are frequent. Palmerín agrees to undertake the cause of a "dueña de mediana edad," who has sought shelter in the house of an old knight. She enlists his aid because she recognizes him and is aware of his fame.

> Acabada la cena, estando entramos platicando en cosas del tiempo, entró una dueña de mediana edad ... El de la Fortuna, pareciéndole que alguna cosa le hacía triste, le preguntó si traía algún descontento; la dueña puso los ojos en él, y viendo á las espaldas colgado el escudo con la devisa de la Fortuna tan temida y nombrada por el mundo, se echó a sus pies con muy muchas lágrimas, diciendo: "Señor, agora creo que mi ventura, enojada de cuantos males me tiene hechos, me quiere favorecer en tan grande necessidad, pues aquí fui á hallar el mejor remedio que podía tener ...

> vengarme de tamaño mal, determiné buscaros á vos, porque
> me dicen que sólo en vuestras manos está la cierta venganza
> que yo espero, é puesto que nunca os vi, bien veo que la
> devisa me dice que sois el famoso caballero que por el mun-
> do tan altamente se nombra" (I.35.59-60).

Her *cuita* consists in having had her only son slain in a battle
over a *doncella*. Despite the story's being a hoax, it demonstrates the
typical characteristics we have been describing in similar encounters:
a troubled *dueña* seeks the aid of a knight because of his fame; she
throws herself at the knight's feet, making an outward show of her
affliction. Here we note that she enters the house after dinner is over.

Another case is that of a *dueña,* accompanied by her daughter,
who is being abducted by Filistor. Although she does not seek out
Palmerín, there are typical elements. The *dueña* and her daughter
pass by el Caballero del Tigre (Palmerín), who, seeing their distress,
offers his aid. Although he is victorious, the girl, having feared a
defeat, has fled:

> La dueña, viendo sus enemigos desbaratados y hallando
> su hija menos, no supo cuál tuviesse en más, el placer de
> la vitoria ó el pesar de la hija perdida; echándose á los pies
> del caballero del Tigre, con palabras y ofrescimientos mos-
> traba agradecelle tan gran merced, rogándole que pues con
> tanto trabajo la librara de sus contrarios, la ayudase á cobrar
> á su hija, que sin ella el vencimiento dellos sería de poca
> alegría (II.4.196).

This episode is not as extensive as others, and does not present all
the stylizing details; nonetheless, the *dueña* needing aid is presented
as a concerned mother. Her grief is visible, and she casts herself at
the feet of the knight.

The *doncella* appears in various typical situations in the *Palmerín
de Inglaterra*. The wandering *doncella* and *doncella*-in-distress are
frequent topics. These *doncellas,* as in *Amadís de Gaula,* may be
independent, or may be in the service of a lady. There are many
references to wandering *doncellas*. For instance, they may be depicted
as being in search of adventure alongside the knights:

> Las nuevas de su pérdida [la de don Duardos] corrieron
> por todas las cortes de los príncipes ... en los cuales era la
> tristeza tan general, que con igual voluntad partían á bus-

callo, poniendo sus personas á los peligros de que ya estaban apartadas, porque el amor que á don Duardos tenían
no consentía otro reposo; y desta manera eran tan poblados
los caminos y florestas de caballeros andantes y doncellas
hermosas que esta aventura seguían, tanto que en nengún
tiempo las armas en mayor reputación fueron tenidas . . .
(I.5.12).

Dueñas are not mentioned as being among those nobles in search of
Don Duardos. It is only the *doncellas* who have the freedom to wander about in search of adventure. It is not fitting for *dueñas*, either
ladies or ladies-in-waiting, to be engaged in such enterprises.

Wandering *doncellas* on palfreys may suddenly appear at court,
or on the road with mysterious errands or messages. Palmerín has
many encounters with *doncellas*. His future is prognosticated by a
doncella sent for this purpose by Daliarte (I.10.16); *doncellas* bring
to him, take back and finally return the magic shield sent him by
Daliarte (I.13.25, I.33.54, I.41.72). These *doncellas* do not have major
roles. They come and go; their frequent appearances are topical
rather than thematic.

Scenes depicting *doncellas*-in-distress are more protracted and
significant. For instance, the *doncellas* saved from a giant by the Caballero del Salvaje suggest he go to England to aid in the search for
Duardos (I.27.46). A typical case in many respects would be that of
the *doncella* who seeks his aid in escaping three would-be assailants:

> . . . Assí siguió el camino de Londres [el caballero del
> Salvaje] para ir á ver al rey Fadrique . . . vio venir una don-
> cella hacia sí en un palafrén, descabellada, las ropas mal
> compuestas, la color mudada como quien de algún dolor ó
> temor venía traspasada, hinchendo la floresta de gritos, tra-
> yendo la voz ronca y cansada, que era señal de haber dado
> muchos y ser nacidos de cosa que le mucho dolía; la cual,
> en tanto que le vio, se allegó diciendo: "Pídoos, señor ca-
> ballero, por lo que debéis a la orden que seguís, que me
> amparéis, que por fuerza quieren robar mi honrra." El ca-
> ballero del Salvaje, viendo que el otro venía tras ella armado
> de todas armas, salió á recebille, diciendo: "Mal empleadas
> sean en vos las armas, pues trayéndolas para defender mu-
> jeres, ellas son ofendidas de vos" (I.34.56).

The adventure, a hoax, is quite stylized. The particular *doncella* engaging the knight in an adventure is a wandering *doncella* on a pal-

frey. It is typical of *doncella*-in-distress episodes that she should have her clothing in disarray, and be screaming. The topic of knights being pledged to protect women (here *mujeres,* rather than the more usual *dueñas* and *doncellas*) is brought up by the knight. There are many such adventures, all demonstrating similar features. Since we have dealt with the theme extensively in other romances, I do not believe it is necessary to pursue it further here.

A more important role is played by *doncellas* as messengers and intermediaries. The Doncella de Tracia has a most important role. She tests the knights of Constantinople with the adventure of the cup, to determine which one should undertake the disenchantment of Leonora of Tracia (Chapter 90). She guides Palmerín to Tracia (101.185-186 and 97.177). It is also she who recounts at court the successful completion of the adventure (II.3.193).

The *doncella* Dramaciana [51] acts as intermediary for Polinarda and Palmerín, arranging a nocturnal meeting at a garden window for the two (I.95.172-173 and II.34.282-283).

Attendant *dueñas,* who traditionally do not stand out from their background roles, have some mention in the *Palmerín.* They are slightly more than figures, but are not characters. For example, we have already mentioned Colambrar's *dueña,* who has a speaking role and brings up the topic of knights' duties (II.232-233). Another *dueña* chastises Floramán for his unintentional slight to her lady:

> El príncipe Floramán de Cerdeña ... atravessando estos días á Francia ... una tarde, ya que el sol se quería po- ner ... encontró con una doncella ricamente ataviada, acom- pañada de dos dueñas, que al passar se quitó el antifaz que llevaba ... y le compuso como quien desea ser vista dél ... Como Floramán, de andar siempre enlevado en lo que per- diera diesse poca fe de lo que passaba por el camino, passó adelante, sin acordarse de saludalla ni hacer la cortesía que a una dama en todo tiempo y lugar se le debe. No tardó mucho que una de las dueñas se volvió a él, diciendo: "Se- ñor caballero, quería saber de vos si vistes aquella señora por quien passastes, ó qué razón tuvistes para no le agra- descer la cortesía con que os trató; si es de no sabella sen- tir, podéis os ir en buen hora, que assaz desculpa es á quien

---

[51] While Dramaciana is not specifically called "doncella," she is the "ca- marera" of her lady; she is not married at this time and would therefore properly be termed doncella."

> no hace lo que debe no saber sentir lo que hace; si por
> ventura os lo hace hacer mal tratamiento de algún dolor que
> os acompaña, de que assaz se parece en los meneos con que
> camináis, mi señora os ruega que por esta noche queráis
> reposar en un su castillo para donde camina, á donde se os
> hará todo el remedio que fuere posible (II.36.289).

The length of the *dueña*'s speech is interesting. Considering the colorless role generally assigned to *dueñas,* the words of this *dueña*
represent quite a blossoming out. It appears that the author is beginning to place more emphasis on attendant *dueñas* than was previously customary. The same phenomenon may be seen in the curious
case of a *dueña* who masquerades as a *doncella* in the "Adventure
of the Four *Doncellas*." She appears on the field in the Valley of
the Four Damsels, demanding that her beauty be defended against
that of the damsels.

> Esta mujer era la dueña que el día de las justas entraba
> y salía en el campo á socorrer los vencidos, que como en la
> corte hubiesse nuevas de las maravillas que se hacían en el
> campo, habiendo algunos caballeros que delante las damas
> la querían desminuir, ella, que viera más del estraño que
> ellos, por ser llegados á la corte de nuevo, pidió á los cuatro
> más esforzados quisiesen por amor della irse a probar el del
> valle, de que cada uno fue contento. Mas el rey, que le
> pesó, por lo que conocía dellos y del otro, no les dio licen-
> cia para más que para justar. Á esta causa la dueña, que
> representaba doncella, pidió justa solamente (II.43.311).

Evidently, this sort of adventure is fitting only for a *doncella*. The
situation is stylized to such an extent, that should a *dueña,* for some
reason, be made to intervene, she must appear as a *doncella*.

We might also point out the use of 'dama' in the last two quotations. 'Dama' did not appear in the earlier prose romances we have
studied in this Chapter. Used in the *Palmerín* sporadically for both
'lady' and 'ladies-in-waiting,' it would seem to be characteristic of the
displacement process we mentioned at the beginning of the Chapter.

VIII. *The Modern* Dueña

Up to this point we have analyzed the role of the *dueña,* lady and
lady-in-waiting, as she appears in the *Cantar de mío Cid* and the
Castilian prose romances. However, an altogether different kind of

figure may also come to mind when we think of *dueñas*: a more familiar *dueña,* the servant of Spanish homes, is depicted in the works of Cervantes and his contemporaries. No direct connection exists between the figures of the romances and these later *dueñas.* The literary *dueña* appears in the prose romances, is developed to a certain stage and apparently disappears as no more romances are written or published. The figure of the *dueña* as she appears in the works of Cervantes and Mateo Alemán's *Guzmán de Alfarache* (1599) owes nothing to the stylized and archaic literary *dueña,* but rather, seems to me to be derived from contemporary society. While the *dueña* is mentioned in some places, she is not found in the works of authors of any importance, nor given significant treatment where she does appear, before Cervantes. From my investigation we can hardly say there were precedents.

The sudden emergence of the *dueña de servicio* as a negative and often comic type in the literature of the late sixteenth and seventeenth centuries poses a problem. Are we to assume that our authors seized upon the figure as a type drawn exclusively from contemporary society or can we find precedents in the literature of the early sixteenth century? It has not been within the scope of my thesis to investigate comparable figures in genres other than the chivalric romances prior to 1599. However, a few statements, necessarily conjectural, seem called for at this point. If we were to search for literary antecedents of the *dueña* as she appeared before 1599, where would we look? Chivalric romance was the genre probably most removed from contemporary reality. There are other genres closer to reality. The drama, with its abundance of servants, would seem promising. Yet the evidence does not appear to support the assumption. I have been unable to find in the pre-*lopista* theater a figure comparable to the *dueña.* In the *comedias* of Torres Naharro I have seen, for instance, we find mention of *pages, siervos, servidores, camareras, doncellas, criadas,* but no *dueñas.* In the works of Lope de Rueda we also find *criados, criadas, lacayos* and *pajes* as servants, but *dueña* is mentioned only in the archaic sense of woman ("Agora yo me maravillo si algunas dueñas de las antiguas se buscaron la muerte, agora con fuego, agora con hierro..."). [52] The only figure perhaps

---

[52] Lope de Rueda, *Comedia llamada Medora, Teatro completo* (Barcelona, 1967), Scena Primera, p. 282.

related to the *dueña* who was to appear later is the "vieja" Ximena de Peñalosa, of the *Comedia llamada Eufemia,* and she is called "ama." Peñalosa appears at the opening of Scene I where she is part of the comic passages as a foil for the simple Melchior. [53] The brevity of her role prevents us from concluding that she might typify the *dueña.* However, there are points of contact. Peñalosa, with her reported boastfulness about her lineage, her complaints and her quarrelsomeness, may be said to have some of the defects of the *dueña* as portrayed later by Cervantes and his contemporaries.

Since the *dueña* was also portrayed as a *tercera,* it would seem logical to look into the continuations of the *Celestina* as a possible source of literary precedents. I have failed to find any *dueñas* in the works I have consulted. The "Celestinas" of the *Segunda comedia de Celestina* and the *Tragicomedia de Lisandro y Roselia* are not *dueñas de servicio,* for they are not household servants. Silva's Celestina is called "honrada dueña" only in the archaic sense. The female servants are unmarried "criadas" or "doncellas." Until a more thoroughgoing investigation of the subject is made, we must conclude from the evidence at hand that the *dueña de servicio* does not appear as a literary type or character until the late sixteenth century, and that when she finally did appear the authors gathered their material largely from contemporary reality. It may be that until mid-sixteenth century the *dueña* held a position only in the homes of the high nobility and was much less likely to become an object of satire.

---

[53] Scena Primera, pp. 47-62.

CHAPTER III

THE *DUEÑA* IN THE WORKS OF CERVANTES AND HIS CONTEMPORARIES

I. The Dueña *of Society and Literature*

Why did the *dueña* become so popular a figure in the literature of the late sixteenth and seventeenth centuries? [1] Already a proverbial figure in the sixteenth century, [2] she later appeared as a negative

---

[1] By the late sixteenth century 'dueña' had been all but restricted to denote the *dueña de servicio,* the servant of authority whose task it was to oversee the other female servants of the household, and to watch over the young ladies of the family. The definition of the *Diccionario de Autoridades* (1732) (Madrid, 1969) follows:

> "Se entienden comunmente aquellas mujeres viudas y de respeto que se tienen en Palacio y en las casas de los señores para autoridad de las antesalas y guarda de las demás criadas..."

Covarrubias, *Tesoro de la lengua castellana* (1611), explains:

> "En lengua castellana antigua vale señora anciana viuda; agora significa comunmente las que sirven con tocas largas y mongiles, a diferencia de las donzellas. y en palacio llaman dueña de honor personas principales que han enbiudado y las reynas y princesas las tienen cerca de sus personas en palacio."

The *dueña* of medieval Spanish society (and even less the lady of the prose romances) was not generally remembered when the word was used in contemporary society. The degree to which the archaic acceptation had been forgotten in the seventeenth century is indicated by an anecdote recounted by Rodríguez Marín, "Las dueñas," Appendix 32, *Don Quijote,* X, 67. Fr. Juan de la Cerda, *Libro intitulado vida política de todos los estados de las mugeres,* mentions the presence of a devout "dueña" in paradise (folio 394). The copy seen by Rodríguez Marín had been annotated in a seventeenth-century hand. The annotator wrote in the margin "*Dueñas en la gloria?* linda cosa." He had failed to understand the use of 'dueña' as an equivalent for 'señora,' taking it for modern 'dueña de servicio.'

[2] Correas, *Vocabulario de refranes* (ed. Combet), lists several adages and proverbs clearly relating to the *dueña de servicio.* These show the ladies'

and often comic type in the works of Cervantes and his contemporaries. The unpleasant traits attributed to her by society at large
may perhaps account for the *dueña*'s notoriety as an object of satire. [3]
We can state with certainty, at least, that her detractors capitalized
upon these negative qualities. A survey of the literary works of the
period shows the *dueña* depicted as a gossip, a trickster and a go-
between. She is talkative, sharp-tongued and bothersome. [4] To these
defects we can add, from all evidence, the following: she is vain,
lazy and self-important. Typically, the *dueña* is unattractive, middle-
aged to old, and may wear eyeglasses.

The *dueña* of contemporary society could be identified immediately by her dress. She wore a long, white headdress, a black mourn-

---

faults had earned them a negative reputation in the sixteenth century. I have
modernized the spelling.

Entonces perdió la dueña su onor, cuando habló mal y oyó peor (139a).
Cien dueñas en un corral, todas dicen un cantar (300a).
Cien dueñas en un corral, todas mean a la par (300a).
Dueña que en alto hila, abajo se umilla (338a).
Dueña que de alto mira, de alto se remira (338a).
Dueña que mucho mira, poco hila (338a).

The adages refer to the *dueña*'s nosiness, inclination to gossip and self-
important airs.

It is not entirely clear whether other adages mentioning 'dueña' refer to
the servant. For instance, Olla, ¿por qué no cosiste? —Dueña, porque no
me meziste" (175b) would seem to be using the word in its already archaic
acceptation of 'woman.' The well-known proverb "Ruin con ruin, que ansí
casan en Dueñas" (575a) refers, of course, to the practice of the townspeople
of Dueñas to marry only among themselves to the exclusion of all outsiders.
However, Quevedo puns on the name of the town to ridicule the servants.
"—Mas quiero parar en la horca que en Dueñas" is the punch line of an
anecdote about a traveler told by Quintañona as an example of the ill-repute
of *dueñas*.

[3] Rodríguez Marín observed "Hiciéronse famosísimas las dueñas... por
diversas malas cualidades" (63), explaining the ill-repute of *dueñas* among
Cervantes' contemporaries. Clemencín noted also that *dueñas* were disliked
in contemporary society: "... eran [las dueñas y los escuderos] personas poco
ocupadas, y servían más para la autoridad de las casas que para la comodidad de sus dueños: los unos y las otras eran gente de edad madura, y el
coco de la juventud que solía vengarse con ridicularizarlos" (II.31.128, note).
An author dealing irreverently with the *dueña* could probably be assured of
his readers' approval and amusement.

[4] Rodríguez Marín in "Las dueñas" lists the major defects he has found
attributed to them, and brings together testimonies from various authors as
an illustration. The majority of the works he cites belong to the seventeenth
century.

ing dress and a cloak or cape. A description in the *Diccionario de Autoridades* gives these details:

> ... Estas andaban vestidas de negro con unas tocas blancas de lienzo a beatilla, que pendiente de la cabeza baxan por la circunferencia del rostro, y uniéndose debajo de la barba, se prendían en los hombros, y descendían por el pecho hasta la mitad de la falda y asimismo llevaban siempre un manto prendido por los hombros, desde donde remataban las tocas de la cabeza.

The sombre dress, a sign of the *dueña's* authority within the home, must have been singularly unattractive and little to the liking of the women who wore it. The point does not escape the notice of her critics, for we shall see that *dueñas* are depicted as resentful of the "infeliz monjil," "funesto manto" and "mortaja destas tocas." Doña Rodríguez even says that the "negro monjil" is worn "como quien cubre o tapa un muladar en día de procesión" (II.37.866).

The *dueñas* of Mateo Alemán, Cervantes, Suárez de Figueroa and Quevedo have the disagreeable characteristics outlined above. A study of the *dueña* in the four authors will provide a representative view of the figure in literature after 1599. [5] They depict the *dueña de servicio* satirically, and the resultant portrait is a stereotype. While Cervantes' early treatment of the type conforms to the stereotype, his handling of the *dueña* after 1613 becomes thematic rather than topical, and after 1615 represents an innovation over the view presented in his contemporaries' and his own earlier works.

II. *Mateo Alemán*

Mateo Alemán's *Guzmán de Alfarache,* Part I (1599) furnishes one of the earliest known examples of the *dueña de servicio* as a go-between. A "buena dueña de tocas largas reverendas" is the go-

---

[5] Mateo Alemán presents the *dueña* as a go-between, while Quevedo elaborates a caricature of the servant in the person of Quintañona. Suárez de Figueroa, in depicting his *dueña* as a member of the household, furnishes us with a more complete picture of the *dueña* than is found in the works of contemporary seventeenth-century authors, with the exception of Cervantes. It is Cervantes who deals with the *dueña* most extensively, and the influence of the Cervantic depiction may be detected in both Suárez de Figueroa and Quevedo (p. 66, note 15 and p. 99, note 36).

between in an adulterous affair between the picaro's parents before their marriage. [6] Alemán introduces her with a bitterly severe denunciation of all *dueñas*:

> ... Suelen ser las tales ministros de Satanás, con que mina y postra las fuertes torres de las más castas mujeres; que por mejorarse de mongiles y mantos y tener en sus cajas otras de mermelada, no habrá traición que no intenten, fealdad que no soliciten, sangre que no saquen, castidad que no manchen, limpieza que no ensucien ni maldad con que no salgan (76-77).

His condemnation of *dueñas* as a class emphasizes their venality with the concrete detail of the "mongiles" and "mantos." Accordingly, this particular *dueña* seeks to obtain the young woman's consent for her own personal profit.

> Comenzó [mi padre] ... con la dueña a sembrar, con mi madre a pródigamente gastar: ellas alegremente a recebir. Y como al bien la gratitud es tan debida y el que recibe queda obligado a reconocimiento, la dueña lo solicitó de modo, que a las buenas ganas que mi madre tuvo, fué llegando leño a leño y de flacas estopas levantó brevemente un terrible fuego (77).

The force of the depiction of the *dueña* as an unscrupulous go-between who leads the innocent astray is somewhat diminished by the fact that Guzmán's mother, as the mistress of an old man, could not have been unaware of the perils or implications of the situation, nor displeased by them. The character of the parents is in keeping with the genre. Nonetheless, Alemán's indictment of *dueñas* at the beginning of the episode attests to the low esteem in which he held them.

Alemán's severe negative view of *dueñas* leads us to wonder whether there could have been a prior development of the *dueña de servicio* in literature as a go-between. Whether the author's attitude was based on an exaggeration of social reality, literary reminiscence, or on a combination of the two, is not easily determined. It is fairly clear that by the mid-sixteenth century the historical *dueña* was con-

---

[6] Mateo Alemán, *Guzmán de Alfarache,* ed. Samuel Gili y Gaya, Clás. Cast., v. I, 75-93.

sidered by society to be an intermediary. Sermons of the times, for instance, were known to allege that the devil led women astray with *dueñas*,[7] an implication also found later in Alemán's "ministros de Satanás." This view passed into at least one literary work of the times,[8] and one autobiographical work similarly implies that *dueñas* were thought of as intermediaries.[9] It appears to me that authors

---

[7] See Rodríguez Marín, "Las dueñas," 65. He refers to a sermon of Fray Hernando de Santiago.

[8] The *dueña* as a go-between is alluded to in a fragment of a satire written by Diego Hurtado de Mendoza (Rodríguez Marín, 65 mentioned the reference in passing). In the *Obras poéticas de Diego Hurtado de Mendoza, Colección de libros españoles raros o curiosos*, v. 11, ed. Wm. I. Knapp (Madrid, 1877), pp. 218-219, this explanation of a woman's surprising bestowal of her love on one unworthy of her is given:

> Gran fuerza es la del oro, ni hay escudo
> Ni torre que resista a su potencia;
> Dígalo Danae, pues que yo estoy mudo.
> Pues ¿cómo le haría resistencia
> Una dueña avarienta y comilona,
> Ancha de nalgas y ancha de conciencia?
> Al fin, para hacer dueñas gran persona
> Es una dueña...

The poet, like Mateo Alemán later in 1599, attributes to venality the *dueña*'s motives. While Mendoza does use 'dueñas' and 'doncellas' to indicate mature women and maidens (pp. 121, 163), he refers to the *dueña* as a servant consistently enough (138, 181, 208) to make it clear that he is referring to the servant in the satire. Even mid-sixteenth century the meaning of 'dueña,' 'matron' and 'dueña,' 'servant' could still be the subject of puns, as above, or in the following:

> Importunadla bien, señora Peña,
> Que yo sé cuánto vos podéis con ella:
> Ansí os pueda yo ver tan buena dueña
> Como agora a mis ojos sois doncella (138).

The verses were written to Doña Marina de Aragón's dueña, María de Peña, to complain of the lady's neglect of the poet.

[9] The earliest negative allusion to the *dueña de servicio* that I know of implies that the servant could have been thought of as an intermediary by society at large. Rodríguez Marín, *op. cit.*, pp. 66-67, relates an anecdote found in the autobiography of Alonso Enríquez, *Libro de la vida y costumbres de d. Alonso de Enríquez, caballero noble desbaratado*, Chapter 62, *Colección de documentos inéditos para la historia de España*, v. 85. Enríquez, visiting the noblewoman, Doña Marina de Aragón, in 1543, fears the lady has placed him in a compromising position by leading him to her chapel through long, dark halls to see an altar of which she was especially proud. Upon finally reaching the chapel, he prays for deliverance from the embarrassing situation. Seeing that Don Alonso is visibly relieved by the arrival of a *dueña de servicio*, Doña Marina jokes "Mirá, señor don Alonso, hágoos saber que nunca se hizo mal recado sino con dueña."

depicting the *dueña* drew their material from contemporary society. However, although there are no notable literary precedents, it is possible that the existence of a tradition in which other old women — coincidentally also called "dueñas" — were portrayed as *terceras,* could have provided a climate conducive to the late sixteenth- and seventeenth-century portrayal of the contemporary *dueña* as an intermediary and an old woman with generally unfavorable traits. Fertile ground for the development of the *dueña* as a go-between in literature could have been provided by recollections of Quintañona and of Celestina and her descendants. The use of 'dueña' ('mature woman,' not servant') to designate *alcahuetas* in the *Celestina* and elsewhere may provide a point of contact between the well-established and popular tradition of the go-between and the contemporary *dueña de servicio.* [10]

III. *Suárez de Figueroa*

Cristóbal Suárez de Figueroa, in *El Pasagero* (1617), deals with the *dueña* as a member of the household. The presentation of the *dueña* is therefore more complete than in *Guzmán de Alfarache,* since

---

[10] The following passage on *alcahuetas* is found in Cristóbal de Castillejo's *Diálogo de las mujeres,* ed. Joaquín del Val (Madrid, 1956), p. 251. The first known edition was 1544.

> ... Unas dueñas
> amorosas, halagüeñas
> en sus gestos y visajes
> van y vienen con mensajes,
> más son algo pedigüeñas
> y pesadas ...

While it is clear from the use of 'dueña' throughout Castillejo's work that he means 'mature woman,' and not precisely *dueña de servicio,* the similarity of the description of the go-between in this passage to that of the *dueña de servicio* is striking.

While there are no *dueñas de servicio* in the Celestina or in its continuations, the word itself, in its archaic acceptation, and the circumstances in which it is used, provide a point of contact. Celestina, of course, is referred to as "dueña." For example, see *La Celestina,* ed. Julio Cejador y Frauca, Clás. Cast., v. 1, Act I, pp. 69 and 70, and Act V, p. 201. Cervantes appears to refer back to the Celestina figure in the names he has the servants call Marialonso: "...ninguna la llamó vieja, que no fuesse con su epitecto y adjetiuo de hechizera y barbuda, de antojadiza y de otros..." *Novelas ejemplares* (ed. Schevill and Bonilla, II, 238). Similarly, Celestina claimed Melibea had called her "hechizera, alcahueta, vieja, barbuda e otros muchos inominosos nombres" (VI.213).

the figure is seen in her accustomed role. The narrator, Don Luis, gives a brief account of her duties. She spends all her time "en la sala de estrado, de quien la tal era centinela, siempre ocupada en su labor." [11] The *dueña* is old, and Don Luis describes her as "cierta Sarra en edad" (41). Figueroa stresses her vanity. This "documental Quintañona" insists she was at one time more attractive than her lady and tries to pass herself off as younger than she is (42-43). She blames her present unattractiveness on the unflattering habit worn by *dueñas,* which she dislikes intensely.

> En medio de tantos infortunios, suele causarme algún alivio la consideración de las ventajas que le hice [a mi señora] antes que este infeliz monjil, este funesto manto y la mortaja destas tocas (traje que tanto afea) descluciese mi lustre y ocultase mi buena desposición (42).

and

> Ocultan estas pliegues cabellos largos y lustrosos; lisa está la cara; entera la persona; y si bien la continua labor turbó algo la vista, sólo me sirven los antojos para de cerca; que de lejos no penetra tanto un lince (43).

The detail of the eyeglasses conforms to the stereotype. [12]

Figueroa's *dueña* is also a gossip. She divulges to Don Luis that her lady is stingy (42) and accuses her, moreover, of harsh ways and of failing to keep her word. Having promised the vain and self-important *dueña* she would not be addressed as *vos,* "Voséame sin ocasión á cada paso..." (42). Talkative and pretentious, she seeks to impress Don Luis with her family's social importance. She boasts that among her relatives were "gran cantidad de hábitos, cuatro títulos, dos virreyes..." (41). In addition to these defects, the *dueña* is

---

[11] Cristóbal Suárez de Figueroa, *El Pasagero,* ed. Francisco Rodríguez Marín, reprint of the edition of Madrid, 1617 (Madrid, 1913), Alivio III, p. 41.

[12] Rodríguez Marín, *Don Quijote,* II.48.75, in a note to Cervantes' description of Doña Rodríguez as "toquiblanca" and "antojuna" comments that this was the usual appearance of *dueñas.* Although it is true that some *dueñas* may have worn eyeglasses because of the strain caused by close detail work in sewing, this *dueña* explains it out of vanity and implies she does not really need them. She seems to want to make sure that her poor eyesight is not attributed to old age.

lascivious. The purpose of her attention to the sixteen-year-old Don Luis was erotic. The dismayed youth explains:

> Con tales rodeos y artificios, ya de pasado fausto, ya de presente calamidad, ya de murmuraciones, ya de abonos en los descréditos de la edad, fué poco á poco manifestando mi documental Quintañona que la tiranizaba el amor y que era yo la causa de su incendio (43).

IV. *Quevedo*

Figueroa's *dueña*, comical in her vanity and pretentiousness, grotesque in her lascivious intent, is a caricature of the *dueña*. Far superior as a caricature, however, is Quevedo's treatment of *dueñas* in the person of Quintañona herself. Quevedo writes:

> Con su báculo venía una vieja o espantajo... Con una cara hecha de orejón, los ojos en dos cuévanos de vendimiar, la frente con tantas rayas y de tal color y hechura que parecía planta de pie; la nariz en conversación con la barbilla, que casi juntándose hacía garra... la boca, a la sombra de la nariz... sin diente ni muela... y apuntándole ya el bozo de las calaveras en un mostacho erizado... unas tocas muy largas sobre el monjil negro; esmaltada de mortaja la tumba, con un rosario muy grande colgando, y ella corva... [13]

The reference to "tocas" and "monjil" immediately indicates that Quevedo wishes to present the figure of the ballad as a *dueña de servicio*. His reasons for doing so will be taken up in the next chapter. In the pages dedicated to Quintañona he attributes to *dueñas* in general the now traditional characteristics. They are gossips and troublemakers to the extent that hell itself rejects them, for fear that with their admission "no habrá cosa cierta en el infierno" (265). Having been denied permission to "fundar dueñas" in hell, Quintañona is rejected by purgatory as well. She explains, "Y estoy rogando con mi persona al purgatorio, y todas las almas dicen en viéndome: '¿Dueña?, no por mi casa'" (265). She wants no part of heaven, for "las dueñas, en no habiendo a quién atormentar y un poco de chisme, perecemos" (265-266).

---

[13] Francisco de Quevedo, "La visita de los chistes," *Los sueños*, ed. Julio Cejador y Frauca, Clás. Cast., p. 263.

Quevedo condemns *dueñas'* defects through Quintañona's recital of the trials they are subjected to. She laments that *dueñas* must spend all their time watching over *doncellas,* and must be present when visitors call. These tasks, truly the only justification for *dueñas'* presence within the home, cannot be considered at all arduous. Quintañona's complaints in this regard betray the *dueña's* well-known laziness. They do little, and would rather do less. Further, she resents that *dueñas* are accused of circulating gossip, but admits:

> Pues ¡cuando en una visita de señoras hay conjunción de dueñas! Allí se engendran las angustias y sollozos, de allí proceden las calamidades y plagas, los enredos y embustes, marañas y parlerías... (267).

Dueñas, she claims, are treated badly and generally disliked. Maids detests *dueñas* for standing guard over them, masters "porque les gastamos," and male servants for being chaste (266-267). Cursed with a bad reputation and a pitiful job, Quintañona prefers death to the option given her — because of *dueñas'* unpopularity in the after-life — to return to the world of the living as a *dueña* (268).

Quevedo's Quintañona herself has some characteristic defects. She is shown to be quick to anger and sharp-tongued. Snapping at Quevedo, who first addresses her with epithets suitable for an old woman, she answers "No soy sorda, ni madre[,] ni tía; nombre tengo y trabajos, y vuestras sinrazones me tienen acabada" (264). In answer to a barb directed at *dueñas* she says "Dios os lo pague y el diablo os lleve" (264). Not surprisingly, in this conversation she is seen as a quarrelsome, crotchety old woman.

V. *Cervantes*

Cervantes does not differ from his contemporaries in his general views on *dueñas.* With the possible early exception of Mateo Alemán, he was the first author to dwell with any emphasis on the figure of the *dueña.* [14] The frequent appearance of *dueñas* in Cervantes' works permits us to study the increasing attention he accords them

---

[14] Entwistle, *Cervantes* (Oxford, 1940), p. 69 situates *La casa de los celos* in Cervantes' early Madrid period, 1580-1587. If this is correct, then Cervantes pre-dates Alemán in dealing with the *dueña.*

over the years. [15] The first of the Cervantic *dueñas* is, evidently, the nameless *dueña* who accompanies Angélica in *La casa de los celos*. [16] Her role is not significant, and her lines are few. Cervantes deals with the *dueña* as a topic, exploiting the comic possibilities he sees in the figure. There is no insistence on the *dueña*, and she is not a character. She is a comic type. Her brief but humorous monologue shows her to have some of the negative qualities that will form the seventeenth-century stereotype.

> ¿Quándo me veré, ¡ay de mi!,
> con mi almohadilla, sentada
> en estrado y descansada,
> como algun tiempo me vi?
> ... ...
> ¿Quándo de mis redomillas
> vere los blancos afeytes,
> las vnturas, los azeytes,
> las adobadas passillas?
> ¿Cuándo me dare vn buen rato
> en reposo y sin sospecha?
> Que traygo esta cara hecha
> una suela de çapato.
> Los crudos ayres de Francia
> me tienen de aqueste modo. [17]

---

[15] Cervantes' later *dueñas* seem to have had some influence on subsequent depictions of the figure. Clemencín, *Don Quijote*, II.48.462 (note) has pointed out similarities between Figueroa's *dueña* and Doña Rodríguez. Both are known for their skill in sewing, both claim noble descendency and both speak badly of their ladies. We can add to Clemencín's observations that both ladies explain how they came to enter into service. The detail of the *dueña*'s lasciviousness is reminiscent of Marialonso. There may also be some Cervantic influence on Quevedo's Quintañona. Her irate reaction to the implication that she was old is similar to Doña Rodríguez' reaction to Sancho's allusion to her age.

[16] The question of chronology in Cervantes' works is complex and as yet unresolved. The possible chronology of the works treated in this chapter was determined in the main by a study of thematic development. The *dueña* in *La casa de los celos*, for instance, is an embryonic figure. It seems to me unlikely that Cervantes would create a Marialonso or a Doña Rodríguez only to retreat to a stereotypic treatment of the *dueña* at a later date. Cervantic scholars have tended to assign an early date to *La casa de los celos*. Entwistle, *Cervantes*, pp. 69 and 70, places the work in the early Madrid period (*circa* 1587). See also Schevill and Bonilla, *Obras Completas*, vol. VI, Intro., p. 110 and Schevill, *Cervantes*, p. 342.

[17] Cervantes, *La casa de los zelos, Comedias y entremeses, Obras completas*, ed. Schevill-Bonilla, I, 150-151.

Cervantes ridicules her vanity and laziness. Her vanity is demonstrated by the lament of her cosmetics and by her blaming external circumstance (the French climate) for a natural consequence of old age (wrinkles). Laziness determines her preference for the soft life of the household — rest and relaxation — to that of the open road and the military camp. A complaining and contrary sort, she bemoans Angélica's refusal to return home immediately and claims that riding has made her ill.

Other *dueñas* of even less relief are found in Cervantes' earlier works. Two *dueñas* attend Constanza's mother in *La ilustre fregona* and act as midwives for her. Hortigosa, Clementa Bueso's *dueña*, has a brief role in *El casamiento engañoso* ("¡Iesus! ¿que es esto? ¿ocupado el lecho de mi señora doña Clementa, y mas con ocupacion de hombre?"). Her lines are used for comic effect. *Dueñas* and *doncellas* attend a lady in *La gitanilla,* but none of the *dueñas* has a speaking role, or is singled out in any way. A biting criticism of *dueñas* is found in *El licenciado Vidriera.* Cervantes refers to *dueñas* as useless and wretched individuals. He says of the Licenciado:

> Con las dueñas tenia la misma ojeriza que con los escauechados; decía marauillas de su permafoy, de las mortajas de sus tocas, de sus muchos melindres, ... y de su extraordinaria miseria; amohinauanle sus flaquezas de estomago, sus vaguidos de cabeça, su modo de hablar, con mas repulgos que sus tocas, y, finalmente, su inutilidad y sus vaynillas. [18]

The best known of the Cervantic *dueñas* after Doña Rodríguez is Marialonso of *El celoso extremeño.* Cervantes portrays her with the typical defects of *dueñas.* Vain and talkative, she dissimulates her age, probably with the purpose of impressing Loaysa. She says:

> ...Y aunque yo deuo de parecer de quarenta años, no teniendo treynta cumplidos, porque les faltan dos meses y medio, tambien lo soy [doncella], mal pecado; y si acaso parezco vieja, corrimientos, trabajos y desabrimientos echan vn cero a los años, y a vezes dos, segun se les antoja. [19]

---

[18] Cervantes, *Novela del Licenciado Vidriera, Novelas ejemplares,* ed. Schevill-Bonilla, II, 106.

[19] Cervantes, *Novela del Zeloso estremeño, op. cit.,* II, 222.

That she is older than thirty we can deduce from an earlier reference to her as "la vieja" (206). Her talkativeness is evidenced by her speech when Loaysa enters the house. Because of digressions — like the one quoted above — she uses over two hundred words to express the simple desire that Loaysa swear to follow the wishes of the chaste *doncellas* of the household, so as to safeguard their honor.

As a go-between fully integrated to the plot and theme of the exemplary novel, Marialonso represents a more mature stage in Cervantes' development of the *dueña*. She is the most insistent of all the servants in convincing Leonora to give the young man permission to enter the house (214); she undermines Leonora's concern for her honor (206, 208); she brings the ointment to Leonora (214, 216) and persuades the young woman to give in to Loaysa's desires (240, 242). She brings about her lady's downfall, not for financial gain as Alemán's *dueña* but for even baser reasons. Taken in by Loaysa's charms, she has succumbed to lasciviousness herself. She plans to receive Loaysa's attentions in return for delivering her lady to him. Cervantes clearly indicates her erotic interest in the rogue (234, 236, 238, 246); for example:

> No quiso la buena dueña perder la coyuntura que la suerte le ofrecia de gozar primero que todas las gracias que esta se imaginaua que deuia tener el musico... (234)

and

> Llegose en esto el dia, y cogio a los nueuos adulteros enlazados en la red de sus braços; desperto Marialonso, y quiso acudir por lo que a su parecer le tocaua; pero viendo que era tarde, quiso dexarlo para la venidera noche (246).

In conspiring to hand over her lady to Loaysa, Marialonso violates the spirit and the letter of the very oath she herself had made Loaysa take before entering the house. It seems to be the hypocrisy explicit in the deceptive grave and honorable appearance of the *dueña* — symbolized in her dress — contrasted with the interior reality, that so outrages Cervantes:

> ¡O dueñas, nacidas y vsadas en el mundo para perdicion de mil recatadas y buenas intenciones! ¡O luengas y repulgadas tocas, escogidas para autorizar las salas y los estrados

de señoras principales, y quan al reues de lo que deuiades
vsais de vuestro casi ya forçoso oficio! (240).

An earlier version of *El celoso extremeño* permits us to see the
increasing importance Cervantes places on the *dueña* as a character.
The *dueña* as she appeared in *La casa de los celos* and elsewhere
prior to 1606 is a type unrelated to plot or theme. In comparison,
there is considerable advancement in Cervantes' treatment of the
dueña in the Porras manuscript of *El celoso extremeño* (*circa* 1606).
The role of the go-between, a Cervantic addition to the traditional
theme of the jealous old man, is delineated in embryonic form in
"El viejo celoso." When Cervantes reworks the theme in *El celoso
extremeño* the original role of the neighbor Hortigosa is taken over
by a *dueña*. [20] We find that the *dueña* is no longer a mere figure used
for comic effect, but a character fully integrated to the work. The
role of the *dueña* González, as the go-between who convinces Isabela
to grant Loaysa his wishes, is of capital importance. A collation of
the 1606 and 1613 versions shows, moreover, that in the later version Cervantes expanded the *dueña*'s role significantly.

One of the most striking differences between the two versions
with respect to the *dueña* is the time and manner of her introduction
as a character. In 1606 the *dueña* does not appear until the story is
well under way (twenty-four pages into the text), in the scene in
which the servants learn Luis is being taught to play the guitar by
a musician. Even at this point no emphasis is placed on the figure:
"Y dónde está ese músico? ... dixo una dueña" (195). She is one
dueña among several. The outburst beginning "Qué honra? ..." that
undermines the young wife's reluctance to allow Loaysa entry into
her home comes from "una de las dueñas" (207). We cannot even
be certain that this *dueña* is González. It is clear in the Porras MS,
however, that González is the *dueña* who most wishes that Loaysa
be admitted and who carries the ointment to Isabela (215). On the
other hand, in 1613 Marialonso is introduced early in the story, as
the only *dueña* among the servants, and with emphasis on her gravity,
prudence and duties.

---

[20] Hortigosa is also the name of the dueña in *El casamiento engañoso*. The
neighbor Hortigosa is a go-between, but not a *dueña*.

> Y a quien mas encargó la guarda y regalo de Leonora,
> fue a vna dueña de mucha prudencia y grauedad que reci-
> bio, como para aya de Leonora y para que fuesse superin-
> tendente de todo lo que en la casa se hiziesse, y para que
> mandasse a las esclauas y a otras dos donzellas de la misma
> edad de Leonora ... (162).

As a result of an earlier introduction it is more evident from the outset the contrast between the *dueña*'s outward appearance and authority, and her true character, which leads to an abuse of that authority. The concentration of all the seditious comments in the words of one *dueña* rather than several sharpens the negative view being presented.

While there are no substantive discrepancies regarding the *dueña* after Loaysa's entry into the house, the few differences in detail and emphasis are significant. The oath-taking scene differs slightly from one version to the other. As a personal touch, Cervantes adds a bit of malapropism to Marialonso's speech ("... todas las que estamos dentro de las puertas desta casa somos donzellas como las madres que nos parieron..." [220, 222]). The insistence of the *dueña* on being two months short of thirty, a detail lacking in 1606, [21] and her humorous addenda to the statement of her virginity ("mal pecado") make Marialonso a more vivid character than González. The last comment is also an early indication of her latent sensuality. The lengthier dialogue of 1613 is an attempt to personalize the stereotype being elaborated. The change of name from González (Porras MS) to Marialonso (1613), appearing immediately after her speech, suggests as much. González was a frequent surname among *dueñas*, [22] and

---

[21] The Porras MS reads "... aunque debo de parescer de cinquenta años, apenas tengo treinta cabales; sino que los trabajos hacen parescer las edades más de lo que son..." (221, 223). González says she looks like fifty, whereas Marialonso claims she might look like forty. It is possible that Cervantes intended Marialonso to be somewhat younger than González. She is not referred to as "la vieja" as often as González. Perhaps in this way Cervantes meant to make more palatable or credible the *dueña*'s erotic interest in a young man.

[22] Quevedo, "La visita de los chistes," writes "Estaba la envidia con hábito de viuda, tan parecida a dueña, que la quise llamar Álvarez o Gonzá-lez" (218). He mentions only "Álvarez" in Quintañona's laments on how *dueñas* are treated badly: "En faltando un cabo de vela, llamen a *Álvarez, la dueña le tiene*" (266). Sancho, not knowing Doña Rodríguez' name, calls her González to get her attention. Clemencín deduces from these two refer-

its use would allude to the stereotype. Marialonso is a more individual than stereotypic name.

Significant changes in detail are also found in the scene where the *dueña* convinces Leonora to cede to Loaysa. In 1606 González approaches Isabela with "una larga y concertada arenga," but in 1613 with "vna larga y tan concertada arenga, que parecio que de muchos dias la tenia estudiada" (240, 241). The added clause suggests premeditation, and the *dueña's* perfidy is stressed. The same emphasis is seen in the stylistic changes Cervantes made in the following sentence:

> 1606:   En fin, tanto dixo González, que Isabela se rindió, Isabela se engañó, Isabela se perdió, dando en tierra con todas las prevenciones de Carrizales... (241-243).

> 1613:   En fin, tanto dixo la dueña, tanto persuadio la dueña, que Leonora se rindio, Leonora se engañó y Leonora se perdio, dando en tierra con todas las preuenciones del discreto Carrizales... (242).

The version of 1613, with the repetition of *dueña* in emphatic position, clearly insists more on her persuasive powers, and consequently on her guilt. Other details are used to the same effect. The "falsa risa de mono" of 1606, the words used to describe González' laughter as she leaves Isabela with Loaysa, becomes a "falsa risa de demonio" (242) in 1613. Similarly, in 1613 Cervantes adds that the arguments used to convince Leonora were put on the *dueña's* tongue by the devil, a phrase completely lacking in the Porras MS (241). The allusions to the devil, reminiscent of Alemán's "ministros de Satanás," put Marialonso in a more negative light than before. In addition, the change from "vuestro compuesto y casi perezoso oficio" (241) to "vuestro casi ya forçoso oficio" (240), the closing words of Cervantes' condemnation of *dueñas,* also serves to emphasize the abuse of trust and authority by *dueñas.* If the presence of *dueñas* in the household had become almost obligatory, then the individual *dueña* had an even greater moral responsibility, the betrayal of which would be intolerable.

---

ences by Cervantes and Quevedo that the surname was common among *dueñas* (II.31.127-128, note).

The moral of the narrative, which contains a warning against the women as a class, also emphasizes the *dueña* more than the earlier version. Cervantes says:

> 1606: ...Todos los que oyeren este caso es razón que escarmienten en él y no se fíen de torno ni criadas, si se han de fiar de dueñas de tocas largas (265).

> 1613: ...Yo quedé con el desseo de llegar al fin deste sucesso, exemplo y espejo de lo poco que ay que fiar de llaues, tornos y paredes quando queda la voluntad libre, y de lo menos que ay que confiar de verdes y pocos años, si les andan al oydo las exortaciones destas dueñas de mongil negro y tendido, y tocas blancas y luengas (264).

The greater insistence upon the "mongil" and "tocas" in 1613 again points to the discrepancy between the honorable and trustworthy appearance of *dueñas,* a façade or disguise Cervantes has penetrated and unmasked in the preceding pages, and their true nature.

In both versions Carrizales' cloister of his young wife is viewed negatively, and in both the *dueña* is the immediate instrument for her downfall. [23] However, the character of the individual *dueña* is delineated more clearly and more artistically in 1613. Furthermore, the negative portrayal of *dueñas* in general, through the actions of that *dueña,* and through the narrative portions of the text, is made more incisive.

Having seen that Cervantes shows a persistent and increasing interest in *dueñas* in the *Entremeses y Comedias* and *Novelas ejemplares,* we need to ask ourselves why the *dueña* appealed to him as a character. It is easy to conjecture that a strong personal dislike for the group contributed to her frequent appearances in his works as a negative character. That Cervantes had little liking for *dueñas* is more than evident. But how are we to explain his continued concern with the figure? The *dueña* in his early works interested him only as a comic type in topical references. His treatment of her differed little from the treatment he gives doctors or any other unpopular group.

---

[23] I must disagree with Entwistle, who states "...in the Porras manuscript of 1606 there is an attempt to throw on the jealous old husband the whole blame for his wife's misconduct" (96). In both cases the *dueña* shares the blame, and without her persuasion Isabela/Leonora would not have given in to Loaysa's wishes.

Cervantes begins to give the *dueña* more than passing attention, and to develop her as a character, only when he begins to consider her in the role of go-between. Perhaps, since the seduction of a young woman was a favorite theme to which he returned time and again, the use of the *dueña* in this situation provided him with a manner of varying and enriching the subject. Eventually the *dueña* herself, in combination with other elements, would interest Cervantes. In *Don Quijote,* 1615 he brings the theme to its fullest development in a surprising way.

Chapter IV

DUEÑAS AND DONCELLAS IN DON QUIJOTE, PARTS I AND II

I. Doncellas *as a Theme of 1605*

To simplify a complicated procedure we can say that Cervantes explores the theme of *doncellas* in 1605, and the theme of *dueñas* in 1615 as recurrent literary themes referring us to the prose romances. *Doncellas* are introduced during Don Quijote's first sally, when he mistakes two prostitutes at the inn for noble *doncellas* (I.2.43). As he approaches and enters the inn, he imagines himself to be living the experiences he had encountered in his reading. His imagination transforms an ordinary inn into a castle, "rameras" into "doncellas" and the call of a swineherd's horn into the heralding of a dwarf's trumpet. The scene parodies the arrival of a famous knight at a castle as depicted in the prose romances and described in Chapter II above. While the "doncellas" struggle to remove his armor, Don Quijote recalls and recites the opening lines of the ballad of "Lanzarote," which he adapts to suit his own situation. He says:

> —Nunca fuera caballero
> de damas tan bien servido
> como fuera don Quijote
> cuando de su aldea vino:
> doncellas curaban dél;
> princesas del su rocino (I.2.45).

The traditional version of the ballad re-created by Don Quijote mentions *damas, dueñas* and *doncellas,* and 'damas' in this context encompasses both 'dueñas' and 'doncellas.' The ballad contains a stylization of *dueñas* and *doncellas*: that is, a stylization of the traditional scene of arrival in the prose romances and of its characteristic figures. A second paraphrase of the ballad appears in a parallel scene of arrival, this time at a real palace, the ducal palace of Part II. It is Sancho, however, who rephrases the opening verses of the ballad in buffoon fashion as a means of justifying his inappropriate request that Doña Rodríguez stable his ass (31.814). He says of Lancelot, in an improper application of the situation of the knight to himself, a mere squire "... que damas curaban dél, / y dueñas del su rocino." The full importance of the ballad at these two points in Cervantes' narrative has not been pointed out. The rephrasing of verses from "Lanzarote" at both scenes of arrival sets the tone and states the possibilities for the ensuing adventures. In 1605 *doncellas,* and not *dueñas* (who have been completely delected), appear as the theme and form part of Don Quijote's expectations for the events of the inn. In 1615 Cervantes draws only *dueñas* from the coupling, and the ballad now announces the theme of *dueñas.* Both rephrasings occur during scenes of arrival, one at a mock-castle, and one at a real palace, and in both cases the ballad announces the theme that will be developed subsequently.

Don Quijote's substitution of *doncellas* for *dueñas* and *princesas* for *doncellas* in I.2.45 — *dueñas* and *doncellas* respectively being the order found in the better known versions of the ballad — is a quixotic element. [1] Since *doncellas,* who are so if only in his imagination, are

---

[1] The word order *doncellas/dueñas* is found in two variants. Diego Catalán, *Por campos del romancero* (Madrid, 1970), pp. 82ff., contends that, in the sixteenth century, the ballads related to the "roman" or "estoria" of Lancelot were still traditional and could be heard in varying forms. I quote the opening lines of the variants as printed (ed. by D. Catalán) in sixteenth cent. MS (Bibl. Nac., Madrid: ms. 1317), f. 452a:

Nunca fuera cavallero   de damas tan bien servido,
commo fuera Lançarote   quando de Bretaña vino:
donzellas curavan dél   y dueñas de su roçino,
esa dueña Quintañona,   esa le escançiava el bino,
la linda reina Ginebra   se lo acostava consigo.

Pliego suelto, Aquí se contienen cinco romances y vnas canciones muy graciosas, and Tercera Parte de la Silva de varios romances, Zaragoza: Stevan G. de Nágera, 1551, f. xix:

Nunca se vio cauallero   de damas tan bien seruido,
como fuera Lançarote   quando de Bretaña vino:
donzellas curauan del   y dueñas del su rocino,
essa dueña Quintañona,   esas [sic] le escanciaua el vino,
la linda reyna Ginebra   se lo acostaua consigo.

indeed attending to Don Quijote as they attempt to remove his armor, we have no difficulty in understanding the first substitution. The second is less readily understood. Although Don Quijote considers himself so great a knight that princesses would tend to his mount to honor him, he is not a knight and it the innkeeper who takes Rocinante to the stable (2.45). Even in the prose romances only a proven knight merits such a reception, and at no time would so noble a figure as a princess tend to his horse. The *hidalgo*'s deformation of the situation intensifies the comic contrast.

We may well wonder why Don Quijote feels obliged to recite the verses from the ballad at all. He did not cite the ballad as a means of revealing his name,[2] for he says "... la fuerza de acomodar al propósito presente este romance viejo de Lanzarote ha sido causa que sepáis mi nombre antes de toda sazón..." (2.46). Rather, he seems compelled to view his arrival at the "castle" in terms of a famous scene of arrival, such as Lancelot's at the Queen's castle. The opening lines of ballad suggest a typical situation of the prose romances: a knight arrives at a castle and engages in adventures of an erotic nature with a *doncella* or even with a princess. For instance, Perión's arrival at Garinter's castle is followed by the romantic interlude with Elisena

---

Pliego suelto, before 1540, from where it passes to the *Cancionero de romances* (Anvers, s.a. [h. 1547-1548], f. 228v):

Nunca fuera cauallero   de damas tan bien seruido,
como fuera Lançarote   quando de Bretaña vino:
que dueñas curauan del,   donzellas de su rocino,
essa dueña Quintañona,   essa le escanciaua el vino,
la linda reyna Ginebra   se lo acostaua consigo.

Don Quijote's and Sancho's rephrasings (I.2.45 and II.31.814) have variants found in the lines of the versions above. Both Sancho and Don Quijote use "del su rocino" found in the *Silva* and also in the variant of the *Cancionero de romances* (1550) (not quoted here, see Ch. II, p. 19 above). The use of "que" in the line "que dueñas curauan del" depends on the number of syllables in the following word ("dueñas" or "doncellas"). The existence of a variant with "que" facilitates Sancho's paraphrase. It is probable that more variants than are presented here existed.

  [2] It was not customary in the prose romances for a knight to reveal his identity until having proven his prowess and worth. William J. Entwistle, *The Arthurian Legend in the Literatures of the Spanish Peninsula* (London, 1925), p. 251 implies that Don Quijote has used the ballad to reveal his name: "Lancelot... is a precedent to compel duenna Rodríguez to stable Sancho's ass, or for the revelation of Don Quixote's name; and there is even talk of 'the necessity of accommodating the old ballad of Sir Lancelot to our present purpose'...." It is more accurate to say that the revelation of his name was the result, not the purpose, of his adaptation of the ballad.

(*Amadís*, I) and Floriano's arrival at Arnalta's castle by her visit to his chambers (*Palmerín*, I.66.118). Through his personal adaptation, Don Quijote expresses his anticipation of adventures, which, if not erotic, would at least concern *doncellas*, in whose presence he already imagines himself.

Having begun with the scene of arrival as an introduction to the theme of *doncellas*, Cervantes moves on to the parody of other characteristic scenes and episodes from the romances in which *doncellas* appear. The situations he parodies are familiar to us and have been described in Chapter II. Don Quijote alludes to or imagines encounters with *doncellas* as participants in his knighting ceremony, wandering on palfreys, visiting his chambers by night, meeting him at a garden window and "in distress." Cervantes does not handle the theme in the same manner in each case. While Don Quijote may himself imagine certain adventures with *doncellas* (the scene of arrival and ensuing events; the nocturnal visit), we shall see that other situations are in some measure prepared for him. His encounter with the "princess"-in-distress, Micomicona, is fully staged to ensure a predictable response on his part. His meeting with the daughter of the "lord of the castle" by a "garden window," however, is prepared only in a partial sense.

There exists an ambiguity between the "doncellas" Don Quijote meets and the "doncellas" (noble damsels) of romance. Cervantes brings into play the several acceptations of 'doncella' in a series of subtle contrasts. For instance, since a "doncella" in the sixteenth and seventeenth centuries was a young unmarried woman, a virgin, the obvious profession of the *rameras* of Chapter 2 makes its use unthinkable. Furthermore, in no way could they be compared by any rational individual to the noble damsels — ladies or attendants — of romance. It is Cervantes' wit that Don Quijote, in his madness, should mistake "rameras" for "doncellas" of the kind he read about in the prose romances. The innkeeper's daughter is a "doncella" because she is young and unmarried, and Maritornes not only because she is unmarried, but also because she is a servant ("doncella"). [3] Cervantes' reference to them as "las dos semidoncellas" (I.43.478) takes into account all the possible connotations of the word. His usage is more

---

[3] We apply the term to Maritornes by extension, although she is referred to by the narrator as "la moza." Strictly speaking, a "doncella" is a servant in a private home.

than double-edged. Although Maritornes' nocturnal wanderings make the meaning as applied to her quite clear, the inclusion of the inn-keeper's daughter in the term 'semidoncella' gives us cause to wonder. Are we to assume she too has been guilty of indiscretions? More likely, Cervantes calls her a 'semidoncella' along with Maritornes because, although she is unmarried and presumably innocent, she is not the kind of noble *doncella* found in the prose romances. This role is assigned to her by Don Quijote. Strictly speaking, neither is Dorotea, seduced by Don Fernando, a "doncella," although we may apply the term to her because of her age and official marital status. She herself assumes the role of chivalric *doncella* as part of the plan to lead Don Quijote back to his village. Don Quijote, then, encounters *doncellas* to whom he assigns the role of chivalric *doncella,* and it sometimes happens that these damsels are not "doncellas" even in the contemporary sense of the word.

In his exploration of the theme of *doncellas* in the scenes at the first inn, Cervantes juxtaposes the figure as she appears in scenes of arrival and also in traditional scenes of knighting with the reality of the situation he describes to the reader. He identifies the girls as "mozas del partido" immediately prior to Don Quijote's perception of them as "tan altas doncellas" (2.43, 44). Various meanings of the word 'doncella' — virgin, lady — are played upon by Cervantes: "como [las mozas] se oyeron llamar doncellas, cosa tan fuera de su profesión, no pudieron tener la risa" (2.44). When Don Quijote offers them his services in accordance with chivalric usage, with utter incomprehension they ask him if he wants to eat something (2.46). The core of the episode is the mock-dubbing of Don Quijote. He is not a knight as yet, and *doncellas,* symbols of purity, traditionally participate in the knighting ceremony in the world of literary chivalry. [4] In contrast to the *doncellas* of the prose romances, the "mozas del partido" barely restrain their laughter as one of them girds him with his sword at the conclusion of the mock-ceremony (3.54). The fact that "la Tolosa ... hija de un remendón natural de Toledo" and "la Molinera ... hija de un honrado molinero de Antequera" (inappropriately bestowed with the "don" ["doña"] by the *hidalgo*) should take part in dubbing Don Quijote heightens the burlesque nature of his knighthood.

---

[4] See *Caballero Cifar,* 441 and *Tirante el Blanco,* Cast. trans. 1511, ed. Riquer (Barcelona, 1947), I, bk. I, ch. 15, p. 64.

The literary topic of the "wandering *doncella*" also receives Cervantes' brief attention. By way of comments by the "second author," he ridicules their constant wandering, perpetual virginity and the troubles in which they so often find themselves. Don Quijote is the first man of modern times to take up knight-errantry, and to

> ... socorrer viudas, amparar doncellas, de aquellas que andaban con sus azotes y palafrenes, y con toda su virginidad a cuestas, de monte en monte y de valle en valle; que si no era que algún follón, o algún villano de hacha y capellina, o algún descomunal gigante las forzaba, doncella hubo en los pasados tiempos que, al cabo de ochenta años, que en todos ellos no durmió un día debajo de tejado, y se fue tan entera a la sepultura como la madre que la había parido (9.100). [5]

Cervantes is not ridiculing the virginity of these literary figures in itself, of course. He seems to find the idea of their remaining so traditionally, despite the perils of woods and road — another typical feature of the prose romances — humorously unlikely.

Don Quijote's serious treatment of the same topic (I.11.114-115) conflicts with that of the "second author." Relating the pastoral literary tradition to the chivalric, the knight says in his discourse on the Golden Age that shepherdesses could wander freely then "de valle en valle y de otero en otero" and "Las doncellas y la honestidad andaban... por dondequiera... sin temor que la ajena desenvoltura y lascivo intento le menoscabasen, y su peridición nacía de su gusto y propria voluntad." In the modern age ("estos nuestros detestables siglos") no woman is safe from "la amorosa pestilencia" that pervades everything and which makes them "dar con todo su recogimiento al traste." For this reason knight-errantry was founded, "para defender las doncellas, amparar las viudas..."

The syntactical similarities [6] indicate the interrelation of the two passages; the excerpt from the discourse on the Golden Age contrasts

---

[5] A wording similar to the last words of this passage appears in *El celoso extremeño* (see Ch. III, p. 76 above). The expression may be a customary ellipsis, capitalized upon by Cervantes in the two cases, of "se fue tan entera a la sepultura como [en el día en que] la madre la había parido."

[6] Chap. 9: "de monte en monte y de valle en valle" (p. 100)

Chap. 11: "de valle en valle y de otero en otero" (p. 114)

with the irreverent attitude of the "second author" toward the *don-cellas* of romance. The conflict between the ironic view of chivalric convention with respect to *doncellas* presented in Chapter 9 and the idealized perspective Don Quijote articulates in Chapter 11 is undoubtedly meant to be comical. The second passage, however, has a more serious bearing on our theme and on the intercalated stories of Part I. We might say that Marcela, as a pastoral and romantically idealized figure, stands at the pole of the ancient pastoral Golden Age, trying to pursue a literary life, no longer, if ever, possible; capricious Leandra stands at the opposite extreme, infected with "amorosa pestilencia." Dorotea and Luscinda stand between the two extremes in varying degree, victims of "la ajena desenvoltura y lascivo intento." In "este nuestro detestable siglo," Don Quijote notwithstanding, there are no knights-errant to protect them and the solution to their dilemmas lies in surrounding reality rather than in the world of fiction. We could, in a sense, consider Dorotea a contemporary "wandering *doncella*" who has taken to the road to seek redress for the wrong done her. Don Quijote comes to the aid of the mock-*doncella*-in-distress, Micomicona, but he does not assist in any way the "particular doncella" Dorotea. There is a clear, unbreachable dichotomy between the fictitious *doncella* of romance and the contemporary *doncella*.

Cervantes parodies the nocturnal visit of a noble *doncella* to her knight's chambers in the adventures of the second inn (I.16). The topic, which we saw was a commonplace of the prose romances in Chapter II, is reduced to burlesque levels.[7] Maritornes, perceived by Don Quijote as a noble damsel, daughter of the lord of the castle, is actually on her way to be with a muleteer. Her rustic garb is far removed from the delicate silk our knight imagines, and Cervantes

---

and

Chap. 9: "socorrer viudas, amparar doncellas" (p. 100)

Chap. 11: "defender las doncellas, amparar las viudas" (p. 115)

[7] Clemencín does not cite a possible source. However, Martín de Riquer, *Aproximación al Quijote* (Barcelona, 1967), 106 states that Cervantes is parodying Chapter 1 of *Amadís de Gaula* (the nocturnal visit of Elisena to Perión's chambers), but is less emphatic in his note to *Don Quijote*, II.48.160 where he cites Chapter 1 as one example of this kind of encounter. This second view is more accurate. Cervantes could have had in mind any number of similar episodes from a great many sources, and he certainly does not seem to be following the details of any one source. He follows the general outlines of such episodes.

makes a point of describing her unappealing defects (16.160). The scene ends in a storm of blows that render Don Quijote senseless.

The same topic is parodied in Doña Rodríguez' visit to Don Quijote's chambers in II.48. In both episodes the topic is alluded to in the larger context of *dueñas* and *doncellas,* and both episodes are based on a misunderstanding of the women's motives by Don Quijote, whose imagination distorts the situation. Maritornes has no desire to see Don Quijote at all, and Doña Rodríguez comes to his room for an entirely different purpose. In the first case the treatment is part of the theme of *doncellas,* and in the second of *dueñas.* In Part I Don Quijote anticipates such an incident, expecting his career to follow that of the typical knight of his books. In Part II he has been led to expect the visit through Altisidora's previous behavior. Cervantes approaches the theme obliquely. Through the nocturnal visit he parodies the erotic aspects of the prose romances and the traditional participants — knight and *doncella.*

Yet another development of the theme of *doncellas* is the damsel-in-distress. Cervantes presents it in a structured manner: characters of Part I play the role of distressed damsel in benevolent mockery. Dorotea, a contemporary *doncella*-in-distress, agrees to undertake the role of literary *doncella/princesa*-in-distress, in order to lead Don Quijote back to his village.

Cervantes begins by treating the chivalric topic on the level of burlesque. The priest proposes to play the role of literary damsel-in-distress to trick Don Quijote into doing his bidding (I.26.280). Comically outfitted in the *ventera*'s clothes, he has second thoughts about the impropriety of such a disguise for a priest and prevails upon the barber to change roles with him (I.27.282). With the advent of Dorotea, Cervantes refines the theme. Dorotea, as a *doncella*-in-distress, points in two different directions to two different branches of literature. Dorotea as Micomicona, with her elaborate preparations and solemn manner, is part of the parody of a motif of the prose romances and also fulfills Don Quijote's expectation of an encounter with a *princesa*, expressed at the time he rephrased the ballad. As a "particular doncella" she is an idealized being with a vital problem, but one related to the sentimental novel. It is this second category which most interests Cervantes as a novelist, and he develops it throughout the chapters of Part I dealing with Dorotea, Fernando, Cardenio and Luscinda. The two roles, that of mock-damsel and that of contem-

porary damsel, are kept separate. Dorotea presents a fictitious problem
to Don Quijote, but solves unaided her contemporary problem of
seduction and betrayal. At no time does it occur to Dorotea, as it
will to Doña Rodríguez, to place her private cause in Don Quijote's
hands.

Cervantes does not question the validity of the idealistic view
contained in the sentimental tale he presents. Dorotea and Luscinda
are descendants, at least in part, of the damsels of chivalric literature.
Idealized beings — beautiful, prudent and clever — they take to the
roads for the solution of their dilemmas, and their stories enjoy a
happy ending. Having all but exhausted the theme of *doncellas* with
Dorotea, Cervantes does not again return to the theme with the same
depth or the same interest.

II.   Dueñas *as a topic of 1605*

Although it is the theme of *doncellas* that occupied Cervantes in
Part I, *dueñas* do appear as a *leit-motif*. There are six references to
dueñas in 1605: I.13.127; I.16.159; I.21.214; I.32.347; I.43.480
and I.49.534. All are literary: that is, they refer to *dueñas* in the
ballad of "Lanzarote" (Quintañona) or in the prose romances (noble
lady or lady-in-waiting) as remembered by Don Quijote. Five of the
six present the *dueña* as an intermediary in a love affair between a
knight and his lady. Three are to Quintañona. The *dueña* arriving at
court with an adventure for a famed knight occurs once. At no time
does the contemporary *dueña de servicio* appear, although she is
alluded to on one occasion. Likewise, the *dueña*-in-distress, an important figure in the chivalric romances, is absent in our knight's
encounters of Part I. [8]

---

[8] The motif of *dueña*-in-distress is frequent enough in the prose romances
as to be noteworthy in its absence from *Don Quijote*, Part I. It does figure
prominently in Part II. The literary chivalric code demands that knights
come to the aid of both *dueñas* and *doncellas*. For example, Amadís is
identified by one *dueña*, Arcalaus' wife, as "...aquel cauallero que a los
atribulados y mezquinos socorre, en especial a las dueñas y doncellas..."
(*Amadís*, IV.130.1304). Old Lisuarte is famed for his observance of this
usage. Queen Arcabona begs his aid saying "...pues que nunca hasta agora
a dueña ni a doncella en cosa que demandasen les fallecistes, no me fallez-
cas a mí..." (*Sergas*, IX.417). See also, for Lisuarte's own statement, VI.412.
Darioleta (IV.127.1246ff.), the Dueña de Noruega (IV.130.1298) and Arcalaus' wife are all *dueñas* who receive a knight's aid in the *Amadís*, as pointed
out in Ch. II.

The first appearance of the *dueña* motif is a reference to Quintañona as the intermediary and confidante in the love affair of Lancelot and Guinevere. Vivaldo seeks to further test the knight's madness with a mischievous request for a definition of knights-errant. Don Quijote prefaces his answer with a rambling question of his own. He asks the gentlemen ("gentiles hombres") present if they have ever read the annals and histories of England. He brings up the legend of King Arthur's survival in the form of a crow, and goes on to say

> Pues en tiempo de este buen rey fue instituída aquella famosa orden de caballería de los caballeros de la Tabla Redonda, y pasaron, sin faltar un punto, los amores que allí se cuentan de don Lanzarote del Lago con la reina Ginebra, *siendo medianera dellos y sabidor aquella tan honrada dueña Quintañona,* de donde nació aquel tan sabido romance, y tan decantado en nuestra España, de

> Nunca fuera caballero
> de damas tan bien servido
> como fuera Lanzarote
> cuando de Bretaña vino,

> con aquel progreso tan dulce y tan suave de sus amorosos y fuertes fechos. Pues desde entonces, de mano en mano, fue aquella orden de caballería estendiéndose y dilatándose por muchas y diversas partes del mundo, y en ella fueron famosos y conocidos por sus fechos el valiente Amadís de Gaula, con todos sus hijos y nietos... Esto, pues, señores, es ser caballero andante, y la que he dicho es la orden de su caballería... (I.13.127-128).

Despite the emphatic "Esto, pues, señores, es ser caballero andante...," it is evident that Don Quijote has not given a really satisfactory answer to Vivaldo's question. Nowhere in his reply do we find what a knight-errant is, or what he does. The response, however, is in character. We would not expect Don Quijote to answer with a historical definition of knights-errant. The question did not seriously call for a definition. Rather, it was intended to determine the nature of the knight's madness, already suspected by Vivaldo and his companions. Accordingly Don Quijote answers with an evocation of literary chivalry. His response is based on a series of literary allusions that enumerates the famous names of the prose romances and calls up their fictitious world, which he takes as historical fact. Don Quijote recognizes the erotic as the kernel of chivalric romance. Thus, he focuses on the love affair of Lancelot and Guinevere, with Quintañona as intermediary and is content to give it as an ideal example of love and chivalry.

III. "Lanzarote" and Quintañona

There are several points to be considered with respect to Don Quijote's reference to Quitañona. The figure of Quintañona is provided by the ballad of "Lanzarote," [9] cited in part by Don Quijote here and traced by him to "los anales e historias de Inglaterra." The opening lines of the ballad, which mention *damas, dueñas* and *doncellas*, are an important *leit-motif* of the novel, as we have already pointed out. It is quoted or rephrased on four separate occasions, and there are three additional references to its characters. [10] I will give the complete text of the ballad as it was printed in the *Cancionero de romances* (1550) in order to show what details it might have provided Cervantes. We will compare these to what he actually has Don Quijote say.

Nvnca fuera cauallero
de damas tan bien seruido
como fuera Lançarote
quando de Bretaña vino
que dueñas curauan del
donzellas del su rocino/
essa dueña Quintañona
essa le escanciaua el vino
la linda reyna Ginebra
se lo acostaua consigo
y estando al mejor sabor
que sueño no auia dormido
la reyna toda turbada
vn pleyto ha conmouido.
Lançarote Lançarote
si antes ouieras venido
no hablara el orgulloso
las palabras que auia dicho
que a pesar de vos señor
se acostaria conmigo
ya se arma Lançarote
de gran pesar conmouido

---

[9] I have not found any evidence to date that the name Quintañona comes from a Spanish prose version of *Lancelot*, as has sometimes been suggested. Clemencín, I.49.457 (note), commenting on the words "Aquella, nieto, se parece a la dueña Quintañona," says "Lo común era que en España la lectura del Libro de Lanzarote (que ahora no se encuentra) ocasionó el darse generalmente a todas las dueñas el nombre de Quintañona." Ricardo del Arco y Garay, *La sociedad española en las obras de Cervantes* (Madrid, 1951), p. 442 writes that Don Quijote compares contemporary *dueñas* to "la dueña Quintañona del libro de caballerías." I have not found the name Quintañona in the surviving MS of *Lançarote de Lago,* and its earliest appearance as far as I can ascertain is in the ballad.

[10] The ballad is cited in I.2.45, I.13.128, II.23.758 and II.31.814. The characters of the ballad are further named in I.16.159, I.49.634 and II.19.719.

despide se de su amiga	ya desmaya el orgulloso
pregunta por el camino	ya cae en tierra tendido
topo con el orgulloso	cortarale la cabeça
debaxo de vn verde pino	sin hazer ningun partido
combaten se de las lanças	buelue se para su amiga
a las hachas han venido	donde fue bien recebido. [11]

We cannot be sure if Cervantes knew this version of the ballad, or another, through oral tradition, or whether he might have had a written version at his disposal at any time. It is fairly clear, however, that Cervantes did not utilize a written or printed text during the writing of *Don Quijote,* but that he worked from memory, as the brevity of the quotes and rephrasings suggests.

We might well wonder where Cervantes found the details he has Don Quijote elaborate in his statements of I.13.127. It is doubtful that he could have made use of any "anales e historias." [12] We may then refer to the ballad as one likely source of information. In the various references to Lancelot, Guinevere and Quintañona, we find Cervantes availing himself of two details found in the ballad: 1) that Quintañona pours wine for Lancelot in the service of the Queen and 2) that Lancelot and Guinevere are lovers. However, on comparing Don Quijote's statements of I.13.127 to the lines of the ballad, we learn that he says more about the characters than is explicitly stated

---

[11] "Nvnca fuera cauallero," *Canc. de rom. (Amberes, 1550)*, (Madrid, 1967), pp. 283-284. Professor Rodríguez-Moñino's Introduction Bibliography provide the following information: the ballad first appeared in the *Canc. de rom.*, Amberes, s.a., c. 1548, gathered from an identified "pliego suelto" (p. 15) and undergoes but slight modification in the edition of 1550. This text also appears in S.l. Miles 1550, ccxliii; Amberes 1555, 242; Amberes 1568, 242 and Lisboa 1581, 242 (p. 98). Additional bibliographical references and versions are found in Diego Catalán, *Campos,* p. 82ff. See note 1 above.

The text presents a hispanicized view of the Arthurian material. The ballad probably derives from a fourteenth-century prose version of the Lancelot legend.

[12] Entwistle, *Arthurian Legend,* points out that "No romance of the Round Table seems to have been directly accessible to Cervantes" (250). The names of Arthurian characters could have been supplied by the *Tablante de Ricamonte.* Entwistle states elsewhere that the *Tablante* is "the only Arthurian or semi-Arthurian romance with which Cervantes was acquainted" (214). He further suggests that Cervantes could have gleaned the titles of Arthurian prose romances, such as the *Demanda del Sancto Grial,* from the same source, and the name "anales e historias de Inglaterra" from any number of chivalresque prefaces (251).

in it. Where, for instance, did Don Quijote get the idea that Quintañona was an intermediary in the affair? The ballad does not so indicate, although perhaps it might be inferred from the rapid shift from a wine-pouring Quintañona to Guinevere's admitting Lancelot to her bed. It seems likely that the conception of Quintañona as intermediary ("medianera") was a popular belief by at least the end of the fifteenth century. Furthermore, it is possible that such beliefs arose from versions of the Lancelot legend circulating in Spain from at least the early fourteenth century. We shall soon return to this point. Don Quijote in his speech of I.13.127 calls Quintañona "aquella tan honrada dueña." He may attribute the flattering adjective to Quintañona because of her association with Guinevere, a queen, or perhaps "honrada dueña" may have been a set phrase. [13] It is evident that Don Quijote is unaware of the adulterous nature of the love of Lancelot and Guinevere. At no time does he mention that according to the legend Arthur and Guinevere were husband and wife. [14] Arthur is twice mentioned in reference to the legend that he was changed into a crow (I.13.127 and I.49.534), but he is never mentioned in connection with the love affair of Lancelot and Guinevere. [15] Is Cervantes subtly suppressing this important detail because it has no part in his treatment of the theme, or was he merely uninformed? It is possible that this aspect of the Lancelot and Guinevere legend did not receive wide circulation in Spain, although it was certainly known. [16] While the poems of the *Cancionero de Baena*, for instance,

---

[13] In the *Celestina*, Calisto refers to Celestina as "essa honrrada dueña" ed. Clás. Cast., v. 1, Act V, p. 201. The denotation is *mujer anciana*.

[14] Don Quijote actually seems to be under the impression that Guinevere was unmarried. Greatly impressed by Basilio's skill with the sword, he exclaims: "Por esa sola gracia... merecía ese mancebo no sólo casarse con la hermosa Quiteria, sino con la mesma reina Ginebra, si fuera hoy viva, a pesar de Lanzarote y de todos aquellos que estorbarla quisieran" (II.19.719). Don Quijote imagines Guinevere to be free to marry the man of her choice.

[15] The ballad alone probably could not have provided Cervantes with this information. Arthur is mentioned in only one version of the ballad as we know it. MS 1317 of the Bibl. Nac., mid-sixteenth century, adds the lines "que mataria al rey Artus, / y aun a todos sus sobrinos" as a second threat made by the Orgulloso (Catalán, *Campos*, p. 82).

[16] A. D. Deyermond, *The Middle Ages, A Literary History of Spain* (London, 1971), says that the Hispanic texts of the French romances were based on the Post-Vulgate cycle. The Post-Vulgate "drops the *Lancelot* branch of the Vulgate, thus removing the love of Lancelot and Guinevere from the centre of the action..." (p. 157).

make frequent mention of the names of Arthurian figures and the names of Lancelot and Guinevere appear often, Arthur is not mentioned as the Queen's husband. [17] Where the adulterous nature of the affair is treated, as in the *Demanda del Sancto Grial* (Ch. 391, 313-314), it is viewed as culpable and not in the romantic terms it was conceived of in the legend. Guinevere seems to be dealt with rather harshly. For example, the Queen's last request before her death is that her heart be given to Lancelot. Although her *doncella* wishes to comply, she cannot find Lancelot to give him the Queen's heart she has carried about in his helmet (Ch. 443, 332). Why should Guinevere undergo such indignities for her love, as opposed to Oriana, for instance? While in the Castilian prose romances a lady may have an affair with her knight, she is invariably an unmarried *doncella* and a binding promise of marriage is given to her. The affair between Elisena and Perión in the *Amadís,* for instance, may be considered illicit publicly, but not before the eyes of God (I.1.21), for the intermediary *doncella* had secured a promise of marriage. Guinevere's behavior, a clear case of adultery, apparently was not condoned in Castile.

How Quintañona came to be in the ballad at all, and why she was popularly considered an intermediary, is somewhat of an enigma. Entwistle seems to imply Quintañona is an addition of the "typical" Spanish go-between to the Arthurian material. [18] The scholar is not entirely satisfied with the suggestion that Quintañona, as she appeared in the ballad, was a popular version of Lady Mallehault, [19] and wonders if certain aspects of the Tristan legend might not have merged with

---

[17] Arthurian names appear in the following poems of the *Cancionero de Baena*: Nos. 38, 116, 124, 149, 199, 209, 226, 234, 249, 301, 305, 331 = 533, 485 and 572.

[18] Entwistle, *Arthurian Legend*, p. 2. He writes "Spain has but little to add to our knowledge of the Arthurian cycles ... another [ballad] gives to Lancelot for ally the figure of a typical Spanish [sic] go-between, the duenna Quintañona ..."

[19] *Arth. Leg.*, 199. It will be remembered that Galehaut, acting as intermediary, plans and brings about the first meeting between Lancelot and Guinevere (*Le Livre de Lancelot del Lac,* ed. Sommer, Part I, v. 3, p. 257, ll. 17-30 and pp. 258-264). Lady Mallehault is present at the meeting (p. 257, l. 39 and p. 258, ll. 10-12). Galehaut persuades Guinevere to kiss Lancelot (p. 263, ll. 18-32). The kiss is witnessed by Lady Mallehault (l. 31), who later insinuates herself into the position of confidante to the Queen (pp. 264-265).

the Lancelot legend. He adds in a note "Brangain is a better Quintañona than Lady Mallehault. She even served wine" (199-200). While this suggestion is one possible approach to a difficult and as yet unresolved problem, it does not explain certain details in the ballad. The ballad's Quintañona is a *dueña,* and therefore, by definition, an older woman; her role was popularly interpreted in the fifteenth and sixteenth centuries as that of an intermediary. Strictly speaking, Brangain is not an intermediary. She unites Tristan and Iseult through an unintentional error, which is not even attributed to her in the Spanish *Tristan.* [20] In addition, she is a young woman, a *doncella,* and certainly not an "honrada dueña." Brangain does not really appear to be a very good Quintañona.

We do not know exactly what versions of the Lancelot legend were circulating in fifteenth-century Spain. The only surviving text of *Lançarote de Lago* in Castilian shows a facet of the legend in Spain that might explain the presence of Quintañona in the ballad, and the popular beliefs surrounding the figure. [21] The portion of the

---

[20] See *Libro del esforçado cauallero Don Tristán de Leonis ...,* Valladolid, 1501, ed. A. Bonilla y San Martín (Madrid, 1912), pp. 83-85 or ed. Seville, 1528 in *Libros de Caballerías,* I, ed. Bonilla (Madrid, 1907), pp. 365-366. I quote from Bonilla's edition of 1907. There are no variants in these two editions.

> "E la reyna dio a su hija Yseo muchas joyas e buenas, e Gorualan y Brangel, la donzella de Yseo, leuauan todas las joyas. E dio la reyna a Brangel vn breuaje amoroso ..." (XX, p. 365).
> "Despues que Tristan e Yseo fueron dentro en la nao, el tienpo les hizo bueno, ... y ellos yendo assi, vn dia don Tristan e Yseo, jugando al axedres, hazian gran fiesta, e no auia entre ellos ningun pensamiento de amor carnal, y ellos auian muy gran sed. E Tristan dixo a Gorualan que les diesse a beuer, *e dixo Gorualan a Brangel que les diesse a beuer a Tristan e a Yseo; y ella tenia las llaues del vino y de los letuarios. E Brangel estaua amodorrida de la mar, e Gorualan tomo las llaues de la camara que tenia el vino y el breuaje amoroso, y penso que era vino e dio a beuer a Tristan y a Yseo dello, e torno la redoma en su lugar; e torno las llaues a Brangel, e a Brangel vinosele mientes del breuaje amoroso, y leuantose e fuesse a la camara,* e hallo por la vista de las redomas que les auia dado a beuer del breuaje, *e fue triste e muy cuytada por que tan mala guarda auia fecho en lo que su señora la reyna le pusiera en guarda. E como quier que ella se touiesse por culpada e se arrepentiesse, encubriolo, e no quiso dezir cosa,* ni dar a entender nada. E luego que Tristan e Yseo ouieron beuido el breuaje, fueron assi enamorados el vno del otro, que mas no podia ser ... (XXI, p. 366). (Italics mine.)

[21] See M. R. Lida de Malkiel, "Arthurian Literature in Spain and Portugal," *Arthurian Literature in the Middle Ages,* ed. Roger Sherman Loomis

manuscript that most concerns us describes Lancelot's affair with King Pelles' daughter. The deception of the knight is conceived and brought about by a *dueña,* who contrives to bring him to her lady's bed. A summary follows:

Lancelot requests wine, immediately after being disarmed; the *dueña* Brisaina sends for wine, which is served him by a *doncella* (Brisaina's sister); the knight asks for his lady, the Queen; the *dueña* encourages him to drink until he becomes drunk; when Lancelot is "fuera de juicio," Brisaina, aware that he believes he is speaking to a *dueña* of rank, and well acquainted with the particulars of his affair with Guinevere, effects a reasoned deception by suggesting he lie with the "queen" (in fact, her own lady); she feigns having secured Guinevere's permission, and leads the knight to her lady's bed. [22]

The passage under discussion deals with a fertility theme of the Grail legends and depicts Lancelot's first visit to the Grail castle; the visit results in the conception of Galahad by means of a deception authorized by the Grail King himself for that purpose. [23] In broad

---

(Oxford, 1959), 406ff., especially 408, 410, 412 and 415. The sixteenth-century MS of the Bibl. Nac. was copied from a manuscript of 1414, which probably dates back to an early fourteenth-century text (410). See also P. Bohigas Balaguer, "El 'Lanzarote' español del manuscrito 9611 de la Biblioteca Nacional," *RFE,* XI (1924), pp. 283 and 284.

[22] The excerpt we are describing here, from "El libro segundo de Don Lançarote de Lago," has been published by Otto Klob, "Beiträge zur span. und portug. Gral-Litteratur," *ZRP,* XXVI (1902), pp. 202-205. Klob presents a French version (Ausg. von 1488, Weiner Hofbibl. 4, C. 16, Bd. II, A.II, v° b f.) alongside the Spanish. A collation of the two reveals some interesting divergencies. In the French text Lancelot merely asks for something to drink, and he is brought a drink "qui plus estoit cler que caue de fontaine et de couleur de vin." The Spanish text specifically mentions wine as the drink, the obvious conclusion being that Lancelot became intoxicated. The French text is logically interpreted as suggesting that Lancelot was affected by a magic potion (as in the corresponding passage of Sommer's *Vulgate Version*). The French text has Lancelot gallantly asking for the Queen before quenching his thirst, while the Spanish text has him ask for wine first and then for his lady, appearing to be less than the perfect lover. The Spanish text further adds the curious detail that the *doncella* who serves Lancelot wine is Brisaina's sister. This is not even hinted at in the French text and I cannot find any way of accounting for the detail. The above are the most important divergencies.

[23] We will summarize the action leading up to Lancelot's seduction with a brief account from Sommer's text (Part II, v. 5, pp. 107-111). Lancelot is at Corvenic, at the court of King Pelles, where it is hoped the King's daughter will have a child by Lancelot to fulfill a prophecy (107). Dame Brisane approaches the King about how this is to be accomplished, and he

outline, it describes the events after Lancelot's arrival at a castle, where he is attended by a *dueña* and a *doncella*, is served wine, and, having been deliberately tricked by the *dueña*, lies with a damsel he believes to be Guinevere.

Who is this intermediary *dueña* whose actions lead Lancelot astray, and how did a *dueña*, contrary to all tradition in Spain, and indeed the entire Arthurian tradition, come to be depicted as a go-between? A comparison of the Spanish *Lancelot* with Sommer's *Vulgate Version* may prove helpful at this point. Brisane (Sp. Brisaina) is "vn dame de si grant aage que elle pooit bien avoir .C. ans . . ." [24] The equivalent in the Spanish version is, of course, *dueña* and the text at the corresponding point reads ". . . vna dueña . . . que hauía mas de cien anos . . ." [25] Brisane is the "maistress" or nursemaid of the damsel, the Grail King's daughter, who wishes to beget a son by Lancelot (108, 1.39). Brisane is probably not of high noble birth, and she can therefore be portrayed engaging in go-between activities more freely than a noblewoman. We have here an example in Spain, dating to at least the fifteenth century and probably to the fourteenth, of an older woman, a *dueña*, serving as an intermediary in an illicit affair between Lancelot and a false Guinevere. The Spanish MS thus contains at least the kernel of the idea that an older woman might serve as an intermediary in the illicit affair.

In view of this additional information connected with the Lancelot legend in Spain, we may now attempt to weigh the material that might account for the presence of Quintañona in the ballad. Lady Mallehault could provide the prototype for a lady of high rank

---

gives her full authority in the matter. She leads Lancelot to believe she can take him to Guinevere. Since Lancelot is loyal to Guinevere, it is determined that only a deception — the drugging and tricking of the knight — can bring about the desired effects (109). The old woman plots to take Lancelot to the princess in a nearby castle (109). There he is given a potion in place of the wine he requested.

[24] *Vulgate Version*, II, v. 5., p. 107, ll. 22-23. For a study of the episodes in the *Vulgate Version* that relate the visits to the Grail castle (which differ from other versions of the Grail legend), see Loomis, Ch. 9, *The Grail* . . . (New York, 1963), pp. 146-164.

[25] "Libro segundo de Don Lançarote de Lago," Bibl. Nac. MS 9611, f⁰ 309r. I have consulted a microfilm of the MS. The Spanish version of these lines corrupts the meaning, with the result that Brisaina is no longer so old that she could be one hundred years old (a stylistic device to emphasize her old age), but makes her a centenarian in fact.

("dueña") involved, however obliquely, in the affair, but we cannot discount that in the romance it is Galehaut, not she, who is the intermediary. Brangain is also a marginal intermediary in an illicit affair, and is associated indirectly with the serving of wine to the lovers. However, she is a *doncella,* not a *dueña,* and the lovers are Tristan and Iseult. Brisaina is a go-between in an illicit affair, and is also responsible for the serving of wine to Lancelot. Moreover, she is described as being over one hundred years old; the word Quintañona in Spanish denotes a woman of that age. [26] Although Brisaina typifies the *dueña* serving in the capacity of an intermediary, it is difficult to overlook that it is not Lancelot and Guinevere she brings together, but rather Lancelot and King Pelles' daughter.

We are again faced with a blurring of the lines of the Lancelot legend in Spain, and a possible merger of some details of at least two of the episodes in his story. The evidence would seem to point to a confusion between Lady Mallehault (presupposing the eclipse of the role of Galehaut) and Brisaina. Lady Mallehault was a lady of high rank ("dueña") and Brisaina was an old woman ("dueña") who served as a go-between. By the early sixteenth century the *dueña* Quintañona of the ballad was considered to be an intermediary and was conceived of by knowledgeable persons as a lady of high rank. This is what Don Quijote understood and, in all probability, what his reference to "aquella tan honrada dueña" signifies.

---

[26]   "En su riguoso sentido parece quiere significar la persona que tiene cien años, con alusion al quintal [one-hundred-pound weight], pero regularmente se toma por el sugeto que es sumamente viejo. Lat. Centenarius, a, um. Gong. Decim. burl.

> De un Seraphin quintañón
> el menor oy blanco diente,
> si una perla no es luciente,
> es un desnudo piñón"
>
> s.v. Quintañón, *Dicc. de Aut.*

The word is not listed in Boggs or in Covarrubias, however. If "Quintañona" had this same connotation in the fourteenth, fifteenth and sixteenth centuries is not entirely certain, but it seems likely that the meaning attributed to it in the seventeenth century originated at a much earlier date. In addition to the example of Góngora's "Décima burla," cited above, we find the following corroborative usage in "La visita de los chistes," in a statement made by Quintañona to the narrator:

> "Dios os lo pague y el diablo os lleve ... que tanta memoria tenéis de mí sin habello yo de menester. Decid: ¿no hay allá dueña de mayor número que yo? Yo soy *Quintañona*; ¿no hay deciochenas y setentonas? ..." (264-265).

We have still to consider why the Lancelot ballad should have interested Cervantes and become so important a *leit-motif* throughout his novel. Even a superficial reading of the ballad demonstrates that the *juglares* conceived the Arthurian story of Lancelot and Guinevere in a humorous light. How could this interpretation of the delicate love affair have come about? Chrétien's handling of the theme left Lancelot susceptible to a somewhat undignified treatment at the hands of less talented authors. We have only to recall Lancelot in the cart. The Queen has placed her knight on trial to test his loyalty. While his entry into the cart proves his love for her, she has placed him in an ignominious position, for he appears ridiculous to everyone else. Her displeasure at his hesitation is yet another test. Because he is so loyal to the Queen, and their love is secret, Lancelot is vulnerable. Chrétien, however, maintained a delicate balance between sentiment and knightly bearing in Lancelot. It is this balance that has been completely destroyed by the tone and style of the ballad. Lancelot's love for Guinevere could have been construed as a weakness by an audience so inclined. The *Vulgate Version* seemed to elaborate on the vulnerability inherent in the figure of Lancelot in having him deceived by the tricks of King Pelles and Brisane; the Spanish text further encroached upon his dignity by having him fall prey to mere overindulgence in wine.

Lancelot, then, long before Cervantes' irreverent treatment — for Don Quijote goes so far as to suggest Basilio a fitting substitute for Lancelot — is a character subject to humorous treatment. [27] The name 'Lanzarote,' with its ending so aptly homonymic to the augmentative ending, would easily lend itself to comic interpretation, as would the idea of the hero's riding a "rocino." [28] Is it mere coincidence that 'Quijote' rhymes with 'Lanzarote' and that Don Quijote's Rocinante is also a "rocín?" In the same vein is Quintañona's pouring wine for

---

[27] Closer in time to Cervantes, in the mid-sixteenth century, Diego Hurtado de Mendoza refers to Lancelot in comic context. He writes:

> Lanzarote del Lago, cuando vino
> La vez primera en posta de Bretaña,
> Damas curaban dél y su rocino.

> Mas, si el conocimiento no me engaña,
> En España no son tan venturosas
> Ni se dan a curar tan buena maña

(Epist. 8, p. 161).

[28] "Rocino" is an inferior horse, a nag: s.v. Corominas, *Dic. crit. etim.*

the knight, a detail that will be taken up shortly. Cervantes exploits
a treatment begun by the *juglares* and continued by popular tradition.
The "Lanzarote" ballad, in suggesting more than it states, permits
an imaginative author like Cervantes to elaborate its themes at will. [29]

IV. *The* Dueña *as an Intermediary*

The second reference to *dueñas* in Part I is in a sense a con-
tinuation of the topic discussed above: Quintañona as an intermediary.
The reference, however, occurs in a treatment of the theme of *doncellas* in the episode of I.16 (p. 80 above). Don Quijote imagines
himself to be engaged in an erotic adventure similar to those of his
readings. The inn is quiet. Cervantes writes:

> Esta maravillosa quietud, y los pensamientos que siem-
> pre nuestro caballero traía de los sucesos que a cada paso
> se cuentan en los libros autores de su desgracia, le trujo a
> la imaginación una de las estrañas locuras que buenamente
> imaginarse pueden; y fue que él se imaginó haber llegado
> a un famoso castillo que, como se ha dicho, castillos eran a
> su parecer todas las ventas donde alojaba—, y que la hija
> del ventero lo era del señor del castillo, la cual, vencida de
> su gentileza, se había enamorado dél y prometido que aque-
> lla noche, a furto de sus padres, vendría a yacer con él una
> buena pieza; y teniendo toda esta quimera, que él se había
> fabricado, por firme y valedera, se comenzó a acuitar y a
> pensar en el peligroso trance en que su honestidad se había
> de ver, y propuso en su corazón de no cometer alevosía a
> su señora Dulcinea del Toboso, *aunque la mesma reina Gi-
> nebra con su dama Quintañona* se le pusiese delante (I.16.
> 158-159). [30]

---

[29] Cervantes seems to lose interest after the line "se lo acostaua consigo,"
for he does not allude at any time to the content of the rest of the ballad.
One cannot assume that he was acquainted with the entire poem or all the
variants that have come down to us. The vague syntactical similarity of the
lines "que a pesar de vos señor / se acostaria conmigo" to Don Quijote's
"con la mesma reina Ginebra ... a pesar de Lanzarote" (II.19.719) is probably
coincidence, or a most distant recollection at best. It is the latter part of the
ballad that narrates a story, whereas the first part is suggestive of a situation.

[30] Clemencín, I.16.32 corrected "dama" to "dueña," insisting that 'dama'
pertained only to the lady of a knight. Rodríguez Marín, I.16.429 objects to
the correction, pointing out that Calderón ("Entremes de las Carnestolendas")
also calls Quintañona 'dama.' Riquer uses 'dama' with no comment. Consul-
tation of the various dictionaries proves only that they disagree among
themselves. Covarrubias would admit 'dama' only for a young woman being

It is the illicit nature of the situation he has imagined, the nocturnal visit of a noble *doncella* to her knight's chambers, usually arranged by the lady's attendant *doncella,* that incites Don Quijote to evoke a comparison involving Guinevere and Quintañona. We can infer from the text that the *dueña* is conceived to be acting as an intermediary. Don Quijote's attitude places the ladies in a comically unfavorable light. Entwistle proposes in another context that Cervantes' Quintañona involves her companions in a comic downfall.[31] Don Quijote, in projecting himself as chaster than Lancelot and capable of rejecting both lady and intermediary *dueña,* completely impervious to the charms of even Guinevere, involves them all in a greater comic downfall. While we do not expect logic from Don Quijote, what he says is important. He alone, here as in I.2, applies the situation of the ballad to himself. The ballad suggests a situation which Cervantes turns about by having a faithful Don Quijote mentally dismiss the ladies from his room.

The third allusion to *dueñas* differs from the others in that it does not present the *dueña* as an honor attendant and intermediary. Explaining literary chivalric convention to Sancho, Don Quijote reconstructs a typical history of a knight's arrival at court, and subsequent events (I.21.213-216). The scenes he describes are characteristic of a good number of prose romances.[32] The heart of the description lies in the love of the knight for a princess, in which a *doncella* acts

---

courted and for a noble young woman. The *Dicc. de Aut.* presents five acceptations, including all those listed by Covarrubias. We need cite only the pertinent one: "Dama. Se llama en Palacio, y en las Casas de las grandes señoras, la criada de estimación que nunca sirve en oficios bajos, ni se ocupa en haciendas de la casa, siendo sólo su obligación asistir inmediatamente a la Persona Real o a su señora." This description fits Quintañona, a "dueña de honor," quite well, and Cervantes' usage is not incorrect. Usage in *Palmerín de Inglaterra* and also *Canc. de Baena,* discussed in Chapter II above, corroborates Cervantes' use of 'dama' for 'dueña.' While 'dueña' would have been more usual and less open to misunderstanding, there is no anomaly in the use of 'dama.'

[31] Entwistle, *Arth. Leg.,* p. 251.

[32] Riquer, I.21.216 (notes) observes that the knight describes the most frequent scenes of the prose romances, and that what we have here could be considered an outline of the plot in *Tirante el Blanco.* Clemencín cited similar episodes in *Amadís de Gaula, Palmerín de Oliva* and *Lisuarte.* An exhaustive list of the romances where the situations described by Don Quijote appear would be long indeed. As usual, Cervantes follows no specific model in the prose romances, composing a compendium of typical situations.

as intermediary. We are concerned, however, only with the appearance of a *dueña* at court:

> Levantarse han las tablas, y entrará a deshora por la puerta de la sala un feo y pequeño enano, *con una fermosa dueña* que, entre dos gigantes, detrás del enano viene, *con cierta aventura,* hecha por un antiquísimo sabio, que el que la acabare será tenido por el mejor caballero del mundo. Mandará luego el rey que todos los que están presentes la prueben, y ninguno le dará fin y cima sino el caballero huésped, en mucho pro de su fama, de lo cual quedará contentísima la infanta, y se tendrá por contenta y pagada además, por haber puesto y colocado sus pensamientos en tan alta parte (I.21.214-215).

The topic described by Don Quijote is that of a *dueña* bringing to court an "adventure," conceived of as a test for determining the most loyal and valiant knight of the land. The details of the dwarf and giants are unusual in that they occur together, presenting a comical visual image typical of Don Quijote's distorted reconstruction of scenes from the prose romances. The depiction of the *dueña* as beautiful is characteristic, and the reference to an "antiquísimo sabio" is accurate, for these adventures are always of a magical nature. [33] Only indirectly does the *dueña*, as the bearer of a test whereby he proves himself, enhance the knight's image with his lady. The *dueña* in this passage is but a small part of a long description, and is not focused on in any way.

The fourth allusion to *dueñas* is made by Maritornes in describing the scene she best enjoys in the prose romances. The innkeeper, his family and Maritornes have difficulty in accepting the priest's statement that the books of chivalry had caused Don Quijote's madness, for they are avid readers of such romances. To refute the charge each one describes to the priest the scenes from the romances that have most impressed him. Maritornes says:

> ...A buena fe que yo también gusto mucho de oír aquellas cosas, que son muy lindas, y más cuando cuentan que se está la otra señora debajo de unos naranjos abrazada con

---

[33] A *doncella* may also act as the bearer of a magic test. An example is the Doncella de Tracia in *Palmerín de Inglaterra*, I.90.158. An old *escudero* brings such a test to Lisuarte's court in *Amadís de Gaula*, II.56.468.

su caballero, *y que les está una dueña haciéndoles la guarda, muerta de envidia y con mucho sobresalto.* Digo que
todo esto es cosa de mieles (I.32.347).

The *dueña* mentioned is an honor attendant to a lady, and is referred
to in an erotic context. While it is not said that she is an intermediary,
the idea can easily be inferred from the circumstances.

Maritornes' description of the *dueña* as "muerta de envidia y con
mucho sobresalto" is a curious detail. From what source could she
have formed this impression? The love scenes of the prose romances
take place in the knight's chambers, and the intermediary *doncella*
is not mentioned after her lady's entry into those chambers. In garden scenes, another typical situation Maritornes may be remembering,
the couple is separated by a barrier. The intermediary in both cases
is a *doncella* and acts only in behalf of her lady's happiness and ulti-
mate good. The words "muerta de envidia" are entirely out of place,
and do not seem to refer back to the prose romances. They seem
closer to Cervantes' portrayal of Marialonso in *El celoso extremeño*
than to anything else. [34] Perhaps we may account for Maritornes' description by suggesting that her own imagination supplied this detail
to an episode she heard recited at the inn. The innkeeper states that
his books of chivalry are read aloud during harvest time (I.32.347).
A recited tale, or a popular oral version, is always open to more
variation. However, we can see that Cervantes is moving away from
a *dueña* of the Quintañona type ("honrada dueña"), and alludes to a
situation he is unwilling or unable to develop in Part. I. We find an
elaboration of the "dueña muerta de envidia" in *El celoso extremeño,*
where the *dueña* in question has no connection whatever to the ladies
of the prose romances.

The fifth reference to a *dueña* is made by Don Quijote in Chapter 43. The episode parodies the chivalric motif of the nocturnal
meeting between a knight and his lady, arranged by a *doncella,*
through the gates of a garden, or the grillwork of a garden window,

---

[34] The situation described by Maritornes is also most reminiscent of the
second meeting of Calisto and Melibea in her garden. Lucrecia is clearly
envious and resentful (Act XIX, pp. 180-182). The servant girl, however, is
neither a *dueña* nor a *doncella.* She is called "moça" (X.57) and "criada"
(X.63).

a motif previously described by Don Quijote in I.21.215.[35] While
other guests are asleep in the inn, Maritornes and the innkeeper's
daughter propose to play a practical joke on the knight. Interrupting
his love plaints to Dulcinea, the daughter calls to him from the hay-
loft of the stable:

> ... Volvió don Quijote la cabeza, y vio ... cómo le lla-
> maban del agujero que a él le pareció ventana, y aun con
> rejas doradas, como conviene que las tengan tan ricos cas-
> tillos como él se imaginaba que era aquella venta; y lue-
> go ... se le representó en su loca imaginación que otra vez,
> como la pasada, la doncella fermosa, hija de la señora de
> aquel castillo, vencida de su amor, tornaba a solicitarle; y
> con este pensamiento ... volvió las riendas a Rocinante y ...
> dijo:
> —Lástima os tengo, fermosa señora, de que hayades puesto
> vuestras amorosas mientes en parte donde no es posible co-
> rresponderos ... si ... halláis en mí otra cosa con que satis-
> faceros que el mismo amor no sea, pedímela ...
> —No ha menester nada deso mi señora, señor caballero —dijo
> a este punto Maritornes.
> —Pues ¿qué ha menester, *discreta dueña,* vuestra señora ...?
> (I.43.479-480).

Don Quijote again alludes to a *dueña* as an honor attendant, acting
as an intermediary to her lady, as in I.16.158-159, for instance. However, it is typical that the intermediary in this romantic situation be
a *doncella.* In describing a similar situation in I.21.215, Don Quijote
used a *doncella* as the intermediary. Why then does he now call
Maritornes "discreta dueña"? Clemencín has suggested that Don
Quijote assumes that whoever accompanies such a noble lady as the
daughter of the lord of the castle must be a *dueña* and *discreta* like
Quintañona or the Viuda Reposada. This explanation is not at all
satisfactory, for the lady in question in his earlier description of I.21
was an even nobler "infanta" and he did not assign to her a *dueña.*
The text, however, clearly indicates that Don Quijote thinks back
to the first adventure in the same inn (I.16): "... se le representó

---

[35] Perhaps the best known of these garden meetings is the one between
Amadís and Oriana at her window overlooking a garden (*Amadís de Gaula,*
I.13.126-130). The motif, described by Clemencín as being typical (I.21.176,
notes), can be found in many other romances, among them *Palmerín de
Inglaterra* (II.34.282-285). The intermediary and witness is a *doncella* always.

en su loca imaginación que otra vez, como la pasada, la doncella fermosa ... tornaba a solicitarle ..." The fact that he referred to Quintañona at that time indicated he was thinking of the ballad rather
than of the prose romances. Here again, I believe, his imagination
is influenced by the depiction of the situation presented in the ballad.
As we said earlier, a knight would arrive at a castle and have erotic
encounters. There is a kind of anticipation on Don Quijote's part.
For him, because of Quintañona in the ballad, the *dueña* is a figure
firmly linked to erotic and illicit affairs. In the first instance, he mentioned the *dueña* only in an image; here, he sees her in the person
of Maritornes. Don Quijote supplies the full meaning — it is he
alone who first imagines the adventure to be an erotic one. The girls
had no specific plan or situation in mind. Cervantes writes "... de-
terminaron las dos de hacelle alguna burla, o, a lo menos, de pasar
un poco de tiempo oyéndole sus disparates" (43.478). Only Don
Quijote, because of his self-image as an ideal knight like Lancelot
or Amadís, could imagine that a young woman and her companion
would seek him out with such intentions. The innkeeper's daughter
and Maritornes merely go along with the fantasy in order to carry
out their practical joke.

V. *Quintañona and the Commonplace*

The last reference to *dueñas* in Part I is a final allusion to Quintañona, once more in connection with the Lancelot and Guinevere
affair, but with a surprising element. In Chapter 49 the *canónigo*
challenges the knight's belief that the prose romances relate history
rather than fable. Don Quijote uses Quintañona as proof positive of
the veracity of the legends and fiction contained in his books. His
lengthy defense (533-536) reads in part:

> ... Querer dar a entender a nadie que Amadís no fue
> en el mundo, ni todos los otros caballeros aventureros de
> que están colmadas las historias, será querer persuadir que
> el sol no alumbra ... Y si es mentira, también lo debe de
> ser que no hubo Héctor, ni Aquiles, ni la guerra de Troya,
> ni los doce pares de Francia, ni el rey Artús de Inglaterra,
> que anda hasta ahora convertido en cuervo y le esperan en
> su reino por momentos. Y también se atreverán a decir que
> es mentirosa ... la [historia] de la demanda del Santo Grial,
> y que son apócrifos los amores de don Tristán y la reina
> Iseo, como los de Ginebra y Lanzarote, *habiendo personas*

que casi se acuerdan de haber visto a la dueña Quintaño-
na, que fue la mejor escanciadora de vino que tuvo la Gran
Bretaña. Y esto es tan ansí, que me acuerdo yo que me de-
cía una agüela de partes de mi padre, *cuando veía alguna*
dueña con tocas reverendas: "*Aquella, nieto, se parece a la*
dueña Quintañona." De donde arguyo yo que la debió de
conocer ella o, por lo menos, debió de alcanzar a ver algún
retrato suyo ... (I.49.533-534).

The words "alguna dueña de tocas reverendas" refer, of course,
to the servant of sixteenth-century society, and the reference provides
the only allusion to the *dueña de servicio* to be found in all Part I.
In this instance, Don Quijote confuses Quintañona, a waiting-lady
to a queen, with an ordinary servant. Clemencín states that all *dueñas*
were called Quintañona (I.49). Yet, the *dueñas* of the prose romances,
and presumably Quintañona in the ballad, were noble ladies. The
contemporary *dueñas* were not. As we pointed out in Chapter III,
they were generally disliked for their numerous faults and were the
object of biting satire. The theme is just barely suggested here; Cervantes makes an allusion and he pursues it no further. We may well
wonder whether these statements concerning Quintañona, attributed
after all to his grandmother, are not apt evidence that, in the sixteenth century, the literary *dueña*, as presented by the *juglares,* had
been converted into a mere unpopular servant in folk-tradition. Was
Quintañona just an ordinary servant — a mere *dueña de servicio* —
in the popular mind? The evidence seems to indicate that she was. [36]

---

[36] Popular sayings and expressions indicate a confusion between Quintañona and the contemporary *dueña.* Don Quijote's phrase "Aquella... se
parece a la dueña Quintañona" seems to be a popular expression. Quevedo
is explicit in attributing to popular usage the expressions he uses with respect
to Quintañona in "La visita de los chistes." Having insulted *dueñas de ser-*
vicio ("Yo creí que el mundo está condenado a dueña perdurable..."), he
explains why he is surprised to find Quintañona among the dead. He says
"Porque por allá luego decimos: 'Miren la *Dueña* Quintañona, daca la *Dueña*
Quintañona.'" (264). Quintañona protests that she is tired of being referred
to in the proverb, concluding "...ruégote encarecidamente que hagas que
metan otra dueña en el refrán y me dejen descansar a mí, que estoy muy
vieja para andar en refranes y querría andar en zancos, porque no deja de
cansar a una persona andar de boca en boca" (269).
It is conceivable that Quevedo's treatment of the figure of Quintañona
in "La visita de los chistes" was inspired by Cervantes's earlier treatment
here in I.49. In any case, Quevedo carries to its full potential within the
realm of burlesque the conception of Quintañona, alluded to by Cervantes,
as a contemporary *dueña de servicio.*

Don Quijote's literal interpretation of his grandmother's statement, with his own addition of the details of the picture of Quintañona, not to mention the image of the *dueña* as *Gran Bretaña*'s best wine pourer, completes the transition of Quintañona from the romantic to the commonplace. It is a short step from this view to the comical and ridiculous idea of Quintañona's enchantment in the Cueva de Montesinos "escanciando el vino a Lanzarote, cuando de Bretaña vino," in the last reference to be made to her in the entire novel (II.23.758). It is the reduction of Quintañona to the commonplace and to the ridiculous that permits Quevedo's portrayal of her as an irascible *dueña de servicio* in "La visita de los chistes," where she is made a spokeswoman for all contemporary *dueñas*, in order to satirize their unpopular faults and ways.

The picture of the *dueña* in the six references of Part I is that of an honor attendant and intermediary. Her image is that of a stock character in scenes depicting the love of a knight and his lady in the ballad and in the prose romances. We know that such an image is really a literary fallacy, for, except for what can be inferred from the ballad of "Lanzarote" and the prose *Lanzarote*, the chivalric *dueña* does not appear as an intermediary in the prose romances, or anywhere else, prior to 1605. We concluded in Chapter II that the *dueña* is traditionally a grave and honorable character in the *libros de caballerías*, and that the *doncella*, by virtue of her youth and closer position to her lady, is always the confidante and intermediary in these affairs. The true situation we find in the prose romances is described by Don Quijote in I.21.215. Contrary to the image he recreates persistently, here Don Quijote correctly assigns the role to a "doncella medianera." The words he used to describe the girl's role ("siendo medianera y sabidora de todo una doncella...") are strikingly similar to those used to describe Quintañona's role ("siendo medianera dellos y sabidora aquella tan honrada dueña Quintañona").

How is this seeming contradiction to be explained? We have already suggested one possibility in the imagined garden scene of I.32.347. Don Quijote's imagination always seems to return to the situation suggested by the Lancelot ballad. In the ballad Cervantes finds a topic he can employ as a *leit-motif*; the ballad is foremost in Don Quijote's mind because it is foremost in Cervantes' mind. The popular belief that Quintañona was a go-between in the situation of the ballad obliterates the figure of *dueñas* as they were actually portrayed in the Castilian prose romances.

The transformation of the erotic situation to a comic plane, with the intervention of a *dueña*, evidently begun by the *juglares* in the ballad, had become proverbial. Cervantes finds the task he has before him prepared at least partially. The *dueña* motif of Part I is a means of furthering the parody of the erotic situations so typical of the prose romances. The topic is not mentioned for its own sake. The references themselves, and their content, do not provide Cervantes in Part I with material suitable for novelistic germination. They refer to a closed situation with little room for elaboration. The literary *dueña* of the prose romances and the ballad as presented in Part I has no obvious connection to the contemporary arena. The stylized situations Cervantes parodied had no relation to universal experience or truths such as we expect to find in the modern novel.

VI. Doncellas *as a Topic of 1615*

We find, however, that ten years later Cervantes approaches the problem in a different manner and that *dueñas* are a major theme of Part II. Events in the ducal palace center around *dueñas,* and hence they are mentioned from the moment Don Quijote and Sancho arrive (II.31.813-814). Sancho's paraphrase of the ballad of "Lanzarote" announces the theme. Pursued in the *coloquio dueñesco,* developed in the Trifaldi episode and climaxed in the Doña Rodríguez episode, the theme of *dueñas* will now receive a very subtle and innovative treatment from Cervantes.

The chapters dedicated to Doña Rodríguez may be viewed in the context of the concomitant theme of *dueñas* and *doncellas.* In Part II, as in the chivalric romances, we find *dueñas* and *doncellas* coupled as figures. For example, *dueñas* and *doncellas* attend the Duchess: "... Todas las doncellas y dueñas de la duquesa la rodearon atentas ..." (II.33.835). They are present when traditional chivalric situations are parodied. During Don Quijote's departure from the ducal palace, "Mirábanle de los corredores toda la gente del castillo ... Entre las otras dueñas y doncellas de la duquesa ... alzó la voz la desenvuelta y discreta Altisidora ..." (II.57.1012). These references would cause Cervantes' contemporary readers, most of whom were familiar with the romances, to recall the numerous similar instances in the prose romances when the coupling appeared. However, Cervantes is being deliberately ambiguous: these particular *dueñas* and *doncellas* are part of the staff of the palace. They are sixteenth-century servants who are presented as literary chivalric *dueñas* and *doncellas* only by allusion. When the Duchess tells Don Quijote "que escuderos, dueñas y doncellas había en su casa, que le servirían muy a satisfación de su deseo" (II.44.909), she is presenting her servants to the knight as figures of chivalric romance. The two "hermosas doncellas" who had placed the cloak on the knight's shoulders upon his arrival at the palace are contemporary *doncellas de servicio* enacting a literary role, for they parody the attendance of *doncellas* to a knight newly arrived at a castle. Their behavior is in accordance with their masters' instructions, [37] and Don Quijote need no longer imagine encounters with *dueñas* and *doncellas* as in Part I, for they are now prepared for him.

For instance, the *doncellas* of the ducal palace, even without instructions or the prior consent of their masters, fabricate the burlesque of chivalric commonplaces themselves, for their own entertainment. The washing of Don Quijote's beard, another parody of *doncellas'* attendance to knights at a castle, is a bold invention of the servant girls, who narrowly escape punishment by the Duke. [38] Similarly, Altisidora takes it upon herself to assume the role of lovelorn *doncella*, such as the kind that typically falls in love with a visiting knight in the prose romances. In II.44.912-913 she and another *doncella* insinuate the stock situation to Don Quijote; the parody is

---

[37] The Duke had gone ahead to give the servants his instructions: "Cuenta, pues, la historia que antes que a la casa de placer o castillo llegasen, se adelantó el duque y dio orden a todos sus criados del modo que habían de tratar a don Quijote" (II.31.812).

[38] It is generally held that the episode of the washing of the beards was inspired by a historical incident related in the *Miscelánea* of Luis Zapata (*Memorial Histórico Español*, vol. 11). Clemencín pointed out that pages took part in the historical incident, but that there are *doncellas* — "mas al estilo caballeresco" — in Cervantes' narrative. Hence, the episode parodies the attendance of *doncellas* on knights in the romances. There is also an example of the washing of a knight in *Amadís de Gaula*. When Amadís arrives at Grasinda's palace, he is disarmed and his face and hands are washed (II.72.786). However, *doncellas* are not mentioned as performing the service.

For a discussion of Cervantes' probable direct knowledge of the *Miscelánea*, and a summary of critical opinion on the matter, see Francisco Márquez Villanueva, *Fuentes literarias cervantinas* (Madrid, 1973), pp. 158-160.

continued in II.46.925 when the knight is made to believe that Altisidora has fainted at the mere sight of him because of her love. Only
at this point is the Duchess informed, and an even more elaborate
pursuance of the mockery conceived (II.46.926-928, II.58.1014 and
II.69.1103-1107). [39] Altisidora, as a *doncella de servicio* in reality,
and as a noble attendant *doncella* in her fictitious invention, is still
not the kind of noble *doncella* who engages in such adventures in
the chivalric romances: the lovelorn *doncella* was, more appropri-
ately, the daughter of the host or the hostess herself. Contrary to
the situation in Part I where Don Quijote took contemporary *doncellas,* who were sometimes not *doncellas* — unmarried, innocent young
women — at all, as chivalric *doncellas,* in Part II real *doncellas* — contemporary servant girls — present themselves or are presented to him
as the *doncellas* of the romances.

These *dueñas* and *doncellas* of the ducal palace are part of a mock-
chivalric background prepared for Don Quijote by the Duke and
Duchess, or by their servants, for their own amusement. A comparison of the disarming of Don Quijote after his arrival at the ducal
palace, yet another parody of *doncellas'* attendance to knights in the
prose romances, with a parallel episode of Part I (2.45), already dealt
with at the start of this chapter, will illustrate several points. In Part
II, Cervantes says:

> ... Seis doncellas le desarmaron y sirvieron de pajes,
> todas industriadas y advertidas del duque y de la duquesa de
> lo que habían de hacer, y de cómo habían de tratar a don
> Quijote, para que imaginase y viese que le trataban como
> caballero andante. Quedó don Quijote, después de desarmado,
> en sus estrechos greguescos ... seco, alto, tendido ... figura
> que, a no tener cuenta las doncellas que le servían con di-
> simular la risa —que fue una de las precisas órdenes que sus
> señores les habían dado—, reventaran riendo (II.31.815).

In the first inn of I.2, Don Quijote's imagination transforms the
two girls he has met into noble attendant *doncellas,* and he actively

---

[39] In one of her last appearances as a mock-chivalric *doncella,* Altisidora
is angered by a well-intentioned reproach of her conduct by Don Quijote,
and she nearly reveals to him part of the fabrication of events at the palace:
"¿Pensáis por ventura, don vencido a palos y don molido a palos que yo
me he muerto por vos? Todo lo que habéis visto esta noche ha sido fin-
gido ..." (II.70.1113).

projects himself into the chivalric situation with his personal adaptation of "Lanzarote." He actively re-creates a situation. Here in Part II the mock-chivalric situation is projected upon a passive Don Quijote as a trick whose sole purpose is entertainment. In 1605 Don Quijote's rephrasing of the ballad introduced the theme of *doncellas,* explored and parodied in the following chapters, as the knight re-created and enacted literary chivalric topics centered on *doncellas.* However, in 1615 a passive and reluctant Don Quijote chafes under the attention given him by the *doncellas.* In 1615 Sancho, and not Don Quijote, actively projects himself into the chivalric situation, in a humorous usurpation of the knight's domain, and inappropriate to the squire. He had, just before, uttered a paraphrase of the ballad's opening verses

> cuando de Bretaña vino,
> que damas curaban dél,
> y dueñas del su rocino
> (II.31.814).

The rephrasing in 1615 introduces the theme of *dueñas.* It is not surprising that Don Quijote sends the *doncellas* away, and, alone with Sancho, reproaches the squire for the scene with Doña Rodríguez, "una dueña tan veneranda y tan digna de respeto..." (816). The focus of the episodes of the ducal palace is to be on *dueñas,* not on *doncellas.*

VII.   Dueñas *as a Theme of 1615*

The theme of *dueñas* in Part II is explored on two levels: 1) the literary and burlesque and 2) the real and contemporary. The episode of the mock-*dueña* Trifaldi — the literary and burlesque level — presents a *dueña* fashioned after the manner of the noble ladies of the prose romances. Trifaldi, a Countess, is made to appear in the ducal palace as a *dueña menesterosa* seeking the aid of a famed knight. At the same time she represents the *dueña* of the prose romances as a lady-in-waiting and governess to a princess. This *dueña*-in-distress is, of course, in reality neither a *dueña* nor "in distress." "She" is a roguish *mayordomo* who recounts his *cuita* "con voz antes basta y ronca que sutil y dilicada" (38.869), in a hoax designed by him to amuse the Duke and Duchess.

The Dueña Dolorida episode (Chapters 36-41) follows the general outline of the *dueña*-in-distress motif of the romances as described above in Chapter II (pp. 38-41; 50-51). A *dueña* seeks out a famed knight to aid her in her tribulations. She is dressed in black and enters the castle after supper; the aid of the knight is invoked and a statement is made indicating that such aid is expected of a good knight; the *dueña* throws herself at the knight's feet.

All these typical elements are brought up at some time in the episode. When the *escudero* Trifaldín announces the arrival of his lady to find "el valeroso y jamás vencido caballero don Quijote de la Mancha, en cuya busca viene a pie y sin desayunarse" (36.863), the theme is evident and the parody has already begun with the detail of the manner of Trifaldi's coming. The Duke is the first to state the duty of a knight:

> ... De mi parte, si mi favor le fuere necesario, no le ha de faltar, pues ya me tiene obligado el dársele el ser caballero, a quien es anejo y concerniente favorecer a toda suerte de mujeres, en especial a las dueñas viudas, menoscabadas y doloridas ... (37.864).

Don Quijote reinforces the theme: "... el amparo de las doncellas, el consuelo de las viudas, en ninguna suerte de personas se halla mejor que en los caballeros andantes ..." (37.865). When Don Quijote offers his aid, the *dueña*, wearing a heavy black veil, throws herself at the knight's feet:

> ... La Dolorida dueña hizo señal de querer arrojarse a los pies de don Quijote, y aun se arrojó y pugnando por abrazárselos, decía:
> —Ante estos pies y piernas me arrojo, ¡oh caballero invicto!, por ser los que son basas y colunas de la andante caballería; estos pies quiero besar, de cuyos pasos pende y cuelga todo el remedio de mi desgracia, ¡oh valeroso andante, cuyas verdaderas fazañas dejan atrás y escurecen las fabulosas de los Amadises, Esplandianes y Belianises! (38.870).

Although the description is a burlesque distortion of the situation, the possibility for a humorous interpretation of this particular aspect of the motif already existed in the *Amadís*. The mental picture suggested, for example, by the serious description of Arcalaus' wife holding onto Amadís so tightly as to prevent his giving a single step would be comical to a person approaching that romance with a critical eye. Cervantes elaborates on the comic potential found already in such scenes in the romances.

The very content of the *cuita* as compared to those of the prose romances is a factor in the parody. The Trifaldi story centers on the *dueña* as an intermediary: Trifaldi recounts a story of seduction for which she herself was largely responsible (39.874). Never in the romances does a governess function as a go-between. [40] Furthermore, in the romances a *dueña*-in-distress encounter may well end in the marriage of the *dueña*'s daughter, arranged as a sign of peace by the intervening knight, but the *cuita* itself does not involve an illicit affair. Don Quijote is asked by Trifaldi to undo a spell cast in anger because of an illicit affair and resultant marriage. While the precedent for a knight's being called upon to break the enchantment of a *doncella*, also cast in anger as a result of an illicit affair, already existed in *Palmerín de Inglaterra* — although not in a *dueña*-in-distress encounter —, in the Trifaldi episode the freeing of the lovers from the enchantment is secondary to undertaking the adventure as a means of ridding the *dueñas* of their beards. [41]

A surprising factor in the parody is the deliberate fusion of the mock-*dueña* role with the *dueña de servicio* of the ilk satirized and dealt with by Mateo Alemán and especially Cervantes himself. This fusion appears first in the Trifaldi episode through the intervention of Sancho and Doña Rodríguez, whose comments in the *coloquio dueñesco* (which takes place between the announcement of the arrival of the Dueña Dolorida and her arrival) put before the reader attitudes that have to do with the contemporary *dueña*, the sixteenth-century servant, and not with the character of the prose romances. Since by the sixteenth century the meaning of *dueña* as lady had been isolated in the romances, it is understandable that Sancho should

---

[40] I know of only one situation in the romances similar to this, and there the *dueña* is opposed to her ward's plans. She ends her reproaches only when she is convinced the girl has abandoned her intent (*Demanda del Sancto Grial*, Chs. 92 and 93, p. 197; see Ch. II, pp. 47-48 above for a full description).

[41] *Palmerín de Inglaterra*, I.90.158-159. Leonarda was enchanted by her grandfather, Farmadante, King of Tracia and a magician, in his anger over the illicit affair between his daughter and a knight. Leonora was born of the union. As in the Trifaldi episode, it is predicted that only a particular knight may break the spell. The episode does not concern *dueñas*.

not have understood the denotation of 'dueña' in the speech given
by Trifaldín. Sancho has confused Trifaldi, a lady, with the *dueñas*
of surrounding society, abhorred by his "boticario toledano."

> ... Yo he oído decir a un boticario toledano ... que
> donde interviniesen dueñas no podía suceder cosa buena ...
> De lo que yo saco que, pues todas las dueñas son enfadosas
> e impertinentes, de cualquier calidad y condición que sean,
> ¿qué serán las que son doloridas, como han dicho que es
> esta condesa Tres Faldas ... (37.865).

Although Don Quijote is aware of the distinction that is to be made
between the literary *dueña* of yore and the contemporary one, the
situation remains ambiguous as far as Sancho and Doña Rodríguez
are concerned. He says:

> ... Pues esta señora dueña de tan lueñes tierras viene a
> buscarme, no debe ser de aquellas que el boticario tenía en
> su número, cuanto más que ésta es condesa, y cuando las
> condesas sirven de dueñas, será sirviendo a reinas y a em-
> peratrices, que en sus casas son señorísimas que se sirven de
> otras dueñas (37.866).

Despite his observations, Doña Rodríguez now continues the process
of fusing the two kinds of *dueñas* with the following befuddled
statement:

> —Dueñas tiene mi señora la duquesa en su servicio, que
> pudieran ser condesas si la fortuna quisiera; ... y nadie diga
> mal de las dueñas, y más de las antiguas y doncellas; que
> aunque yo no lo soy, bien ... se me trasluce la ventaja que
> hace una dueña doncella de una dueña viuda ... (II.37.866).

She too has failed to grasp the distinction. Although Doña Rodríguez is one kind of *dueña* and Trifaldi another, the real *dueña* Rodríguez and Sancho have confused the two groups — they have confused, again, literature with life.

Cervantes' handling of the theme offers greater surprises. Trifaldi
is even given some of the negative qualities that had already been
attributed to the *dueña* of society by Cervantes and his contemporaries. These defects are given to her by the *mayordomo*, her creator,
in his literary parody of an entirely different role. When Trifaldi
relates her story of *tercería*, we find that the *mayordomo* has created

and recounted a situation more akin to that of the *dueña de servicio* than that of the *dueña menesterosa*. We know that the *dueña de gran guisa* who sometimes appeared "in distress" was not an intermediary in illicit affairs, but that, nevertheless, she was presented as such in Part I, mainly in Don Quijote's re-creations of the role of Quintañona in the Lancelot and Guinevere affair, an attitude reflective of popular beliefs originating in the ballad. This view never represented the reality of the topic in the romances. It was, rather, the *dueña de servicio* who was portrayed as a *tercera* in the literature of the late sixteenth and seventeenth centuries.

The potential for the confusion of *dueña/dueña de servicio* was hinted at, but not pursued, in Don Quijote's statements about Quintañona in I.49.534. Cervantes takes it up in Part II. The *mayordomo* depicts the *dueña* Trifaldi as taken in by Don Clavijo, and induced to act as an intermediary, through an inherent weakness in the character of *dueñas* — their sensuality. The "dijes" and "brincos" given her by Clavijo do not influence the *dueña* being portrayed as much as her susceptibility to the erotic *coplas* he sings (II.38.872). As a result, she says "... siendo yo la medianera, él se halló una y muy muchas veces en la estancia de la por mí, y no por él, engañada Antonomasia ..." (38.874). To make the allusion to the *dueña de servicio* more evident, "Trifaldi" hints that such activity as a go-between was not at all unfamiliar to her. Insisting that Clavijo had been with Antonomasia "debajo del título de verdadero esposo," she adds emphatically "No, no, eso no: el matrimonio ha de salir adelante en cualquier negocio destos que por mí se tratare" (38.874). The *mayordomo* is deliberately alluding to the contemporary *dueña*. That the situation he describes could allude to the role of an intermediary *doncella* or even to Quintañona is precluded by the detail of the bribe ("dijes y brincos") and the suggestion of the *dueña*'s susceptibility to sensuality. The unexpected fusing of the two types of *dueñas* in the *mayordomo*'s role is another instance of Cervantes' wit.

It is the *mayordomo*'s attitude toward *dueñas*, a man's recreation of the unpopular *dueñas* of society, that is being presented. Hence the beards: a generic punishment for a generic fault. All the *dueñas* of the palace, and by extension, of society, are punished for Trifaldi's fault:

> ... [Malambruno] hizo traer ante sí todas las dueñas de palacio, que fueron estas que están presentes, y después de

haber exagerado nuestra culpa y vituperado las condiciones
de las dueñas, sus malas mañas y peores trazas, y cargando
a todas la culpa que yo sola tenía, dijo que no quería con
pena capital castigarnos, sino con otras penas dilatadas, que
nos diesen una muerte civil y continua... (II.39.876-877).

Beards, long symbolic of virility and authority, become now, in coun-
terpoint, a symbol of the *dueña* as a go-between, a fitting punishment for her abuse of authority in the service of misguided virility.
The beards might also be interpreted as a caricaturesque hyperbole
of the traditional depiction of the *tercera* as a "vieja barbuda." The
mayordomo portrays *dueñas* as society's outcasts because of their defects, all of which are now represented picturesquely in the beards.
He (Trifaldi) says:

> ... ¿adónde podrá ir una dueña con barbas? ¿Qué padre
> o qué madre se dolerá della? ¿Quién la dará ayuda? Pues
> aun cuando tiene la tez lisa y el rostro martirizado con mil
> suertes de menjures y mudas apenas halla quien bien la
> quiera, ¿qué hará cuando descubra hecho un bosque su
> rostro? (II.39.877).

The entire episode, ideated as a means of entertainment, greatly
amuses the spectators who understand the hoax, and they admire its
ingenuity (38.871). Don Quijote, having undertaken the adventure,
resolves the *cuita* with his flight on Clavileño. The mock-adventure
is resolved in a mock-conclusion.

CHAPTER V

DOÑA RODRÍGUEZ

I. *Verisimilitude*

The question of verisimilitude in literature concerned Cervantes as a novelist in increasing measure. [1] Although he made use of realistic detail in *La Galatea* to create a more rustic atmosphere, for instance, he did not yet, in 1585, question the idealistic view of the pastoral convention on which he based the entire novel. In the pastoral episodes of *Don Quijote*, 1605, however, the convention is judged from the standpoint of verisimilitude: the story of "pastores pastoriles" — Grisóstomo, Marcela — is subjected to the scrutiny of "pastores cabreros" [2] who pass judgement on it from the reality of their own lives and experience. Cervantes more than juxtaposes the literary ideal with reality. More precisely, the posturings and actions of those who would live in an Arcadia of their own making are adjudged strange and incomprehensible by those who inhabit and tend to their flocks in the rural countryside. The goatherds are as baffled by what they know of Marcela and Grisóstomo as they are by Don Quijote's discourse on the Golden Age. The shepherds who compose poetry and music in 1605 are students and the idle rich assuming literary postures. The rustic song of a real shepherd, it turns out, was composed by "el beneficiado su tío."

Other genres about which we might raise the question of verisimilitude are found in *Don Quijote*. The sentimental novel and the

---

[1] For a discussion of the question of verisimilitude in Cervantes see Edward C. Riley, *Teoría de la novela en Cervantes* (Madrid, 1966), pp. 284-314.
[2] I use the terminology provided by Casalduero, *Sentido*, p. 83.

comedia lopesca are represented in the story of Dorotea, Don Fernando, Luscinda and Cardenio. It has been suggested that Cervantes finds Dorotea's assumption of the role of *dama disfrazada* — a favorite recourse of the *comedia lopesca* — as artificial as that of *doncella menesterosa*. [3] He had not entirely resolved the matter of verisimilitude in 1605, however, and he does not question the validity of the sentimental tale. Despite the glimmers of reality and human weakness in Dorotea's personality, she is still an idealized character in a sentimental narration. It is precisely the idealized facets in the characters' personalities and the nature of the narration that permit a happy ending. In 1615 Cervantes can no longer admit this tentative solution: ingenuity is not the norm in the human condition and happy circumstance occurs but seldom. Even Basilio's ingenuity is less than ideal, for it finds a solution to the problem being explored in the "Bodas de Camacho" only in trickery and deception. There is no happy ending for Camacho, who has harmed no one, and sought to harm no one. Claudia Jerónimo takes the solution of her problem of honor into her own hands, like Dorotea, but her rash actions are occasioned by a falsehood and end in tragedy. Her story shows that in Part II there is no reprieve for those who act out the emotions and solutions of the stage in real life.

The stories of Dorotea, Claudia and Doña Rodríguez' daughter all concern the theme of seduction and abandonment viewed from different perspectives. We may say with respect to the first two that it is hardly likely that a young woman would disguise herself as a man and take to the road to force her seducer into marriage or to avenge her own honor, for this recourse belongs on the stage rather than in real life. The same actions that may still lead to a happy ending in 1605 (Dorotea) result in senseless death in 1615 (Claudia). In the Rodríguez episode there are no idealized or dynamic characters who could even conceive of such a solution, and the theme of seduction is focused from the perspective of uncompromising verisimilitude, with a very different outcome.

---

[3] See Stephen Gilman, "Los inquisidores literarios de Cervantes," *Actas del Tercer Congreso Internacional de Hispanistas*, pp. 15-16.

II. *Doña Rodríguez:* Contemporary Dueña, *Chivalric* Dueña

Doña Rodríguez is the only character of the entire novel to seek out Don Quijote in good faith, as a real knight-errant, so that he might right a wrong. [4] This sixteenth-century, contemporary *dueña* thereby reenacts the archaic literary role of the *dueña* of chivalric romance. We may begin an analysis of Cervantes' treatment of the Doña Rodríguez episode in its many complexities by analyzing the character in her relation to the stereotype of the *dueña de servicio* and, secondly, to the theme of the *dueña menesterosa* of romance.

Cervantes' contemporary readers would have recognized a humorous literary topic when, on making her first appearance (II.31), the "reverenda dueña" Doña Rodríguez begins to argue heatedly with Sancho, for, as a *dueña de servicio,* she is part of the literary convention that surrounds this unpopular servant of sixteenth-century society. The Duke and the Duchess have just staged a typical scene of arrival from the prose romances for Don Quijote, in which their servants imitate chivalric roles. In contrast to the other servants of the palace who scrupulously follow their masters' instructions in acting like chivalric *escuderos, dueñas* and *doncellas* while they attend to Don Quijote, Doña Rodríguez, who, we may assume, was given no instructions at all, or, if she was, did not understand in the least what they were about, becomes immediately embroiled in an altercation with Sancho that leaves no doubt as to her negative qualities as a *dueña de servicio.* Her actions and bearing in no way allude to the chivalric *dueña.* The characteristic bad temper and sharp tongue

---

[4] Doña Rodríguez has received some attention from Cervantic critics, but none has brought up this point. Ricardo del Arco, *Sociedad,* 441, calls her the most famous of the Cervantic *dueñas.* Clemencín, Riquer and others are amazed by the foolishness of the *dueña.* They do not delve into her character or motivation. Riquer, *Aproximación,* states that she is ". . . tipo inolvidable porque en él Cervantes ha pintado magistralmente a la mujer tonta y la ha hecho obrar y hablar de la manera más estúpida y mentecata posible" (151). Clemencín, at least, had noted that the character of the *dueña* was well conceived and developed (II.52.65). Unamuno (*Vida de don Quijote y Sancho*) and later, Concha Espina (*Mujeres del Quijote*) also fail to grasp the importance of Doña Rodríguez and the episode dedicated to her. They advance the idea that the *dueña* has allowed herself to be carried away, or "elevated" by Don Quijote's "heroism." Unamuno, furthermore, in stating that the knight resolves the episode of Doña Rodríguez happily, chooses to overlook the actual denouement of the episode.

of contemporary *dueñas,* rather, are aroused in her by Sancho's inappropriate request that she stable his ass, for, as she angrily concludes after giving him a thorough dressing down, "... las dueñas de esta casa no estamos acostumbradas a semejantes haciendas" (II.31.814).

The very idea that Sancho should enter a noble palace and ask a grave *dueña* to tend to his ass is humorous and ridiculous. He surely must have known that his animal would not be neglected and that any doubts should more properly have been addressed to a lackey. His reference to the ballad of "Lanzarote" at this point, however, indicates a perspective for the incident that stems from a more subtle kind of humor. As if to justify this piece of buffoonery, and not in the least repentent for his blunder, he replies to Doña Rodríguez:

> —Pues en verdad... que he oído yo decir a mi señor,
> que es zahorí de las historias, contando aquella de Lanzarote,
> cuando de Bretaña vino
> que damas curaban dél,
> y dueñas del su rocino;
> y que en el particular de mi asno, que no le trocara yo con
> el rocín del señor Lanzarote (II.31.814).

In Part I the ballad was cited in a parallel scene of arrival (I.2). Everything Don Quijote imagined was happening at that time is in fact taking place now in Part II. We are told that for the first time, because of the deception, he truly believes himself to be a knight-errant: he has been received with honor and "hermosas doncellas" have put a cloak on his shoulders. Women who present themselves to him as *doncellas* attend him, and all that is lacking is that they should attend to his "rocín." Surprisingly, it is not Don Quijote who refers to the ballad at this point. Sancho remembers the ballad as he heard it from his master (so he says), in proof of the correctness of his request: since "damas" attended to Lancelot and "dueñas" to his mount, it is proper that Doña Rodríguez should see to his ass. [5]

---

[5] Sancho's rephrasing is not found in any version of the ballad known to us. One sixteenth-century MS and one "pliego suelto" have the variant "y dueñas de(l) su rocino," but his line "que damas curaban dél" has not been documented elsewhere (see Chapter IV above, note 1), nor is it likely that such a variant could have existed, since it would necessitate the repetition of *damas.* It may be for this reason that Cervantes, who wishes to avoid the use of *doncellas,* omits the first two lines of the ballad — "Nunca fuera

But what has all of this to do with Sancho? While in the ballad *doncellas* (or *dueñas*) may take care of the knight's horse, Sancho is a squire and his mount is an ass. He even goes so far as to say that he wouldn't trade his ass with Lancelot's horse, a remark that capitalizes on the comic strangeness in the idea that ladies of high rank should care for Lancelot's nag, who seems to bask in the knight's reflected glory. [6] The situation described by the ballad has no relation

---

caballero/de damas tan bien servido." It has already been established that 'damas' includes both 'dueñas' and 'doncellas,' and that even in the fifteenth century expressions like "donzellas... e damas" appeared. In the sixteenth century, however, we find the paraphrase "damas curaban dél y su rocino" in a poem written by Diego Hurtado de Mendoza (Chapter IV, note 27).

[6] Although unusual, it is not unprecedented in the prose romances that *doncellas* should stable a knight's horse. John Bowle, *Don Quijote* (Salisbury, 1781), III, p. 82, in a note to II.31 quotes from *Espejo de cavallerías*, Part I, Ch. 16 (Medina del Campo, 1586):

> "El Conde passó por la levadiza puente... entra en un muy rico patín, y llegaron a él dos Donzellas, y apearonle del cavallo diziendo. No vos maravilleis desto ca esta es la usanza desta casa, alvergar y servir los Cavalleros Andantes que por aqui passan, y siendo apeado, pusieron el caballo en su pienso, y metieron a don Roldan en una gran sala."

A similar scene may be found in *Tirante el Blanco*, as Bowle also points out.

> "...las donzellas tomaron el cavallo de Tirante por las reindas y con muy gran honra le llevaron a su posada y desarmáronle..." (I.51.65).

The ballad, of course, pre-dates both romances, and the idea of noble damsels' and ladies' seeing to a knight's horse, no matter how famous the knight, would still seem comical to one predisposed to a humorous interpretation. Cervantes was surely amused at the thought, as was Quevedo, who makes much of it in "La visita de los chistes." The narrator meets Lancelot among those dead souls who complain of their fame or ill fame in the world of the living.

> "—Así es verdad —dijo *Lanzarote*—, que a mí me tienen esos [mozuelos] consumido a puro lazarotar con si viene o no viene de Bretaña, y son tan grandes habladores, que, viendo que mi romance dice:
>
> Doncellas curaban dél
> y dueñas de su rocino,
>
> han dicho que de aquí se saca que en mi tiempo las dueñas eran mozos de caballos, pues curaban del rocino. ¡Bueno estuviera el rocín en poder de dueñas! ¡El diablo se lo daba! Es verdad, y yo no lo puedo negar, que las dueñas, por ser mozas, aunque fuese de caballos, se entremetieron en eso, como en otras cosas, mas yo hice lo que convenía" (291).

Quevedo, of course, is taking one more opportunity to ridicule *dueñas* (and Lancelot too) through the lines of the ballad. For a second time we find the author availing himself of an idea perhaps suggested to him by *Don Quijote*. See Chapter IV, note 36.

whatever to his circumstances. He usurps the domain of the knight: Don Quijote has received "recognition," but it is Sancho who puffs up with self-importance. If the nag of a famous knight is so important, why not the squire of a famous knight, and his own mount too?

Actually, Sancho did not at any time in the narrative hear Don Quijote recite the lines of the ballad he rephrases. He did not accompany his master on the first sally (I.2.45) and subsequent references to the ballad in I.13.128 and II.23.758 make no mention of the lines in question. It would be an underestimation of Cervantes' wit to assume that the knight recited the lines at some point not "recorded" in the "verdadera historia." He imposes the citation of the ballad upon his character as an omniscient author. It is Cervantes' conceit that Sancho should bring up these particular lines of the ballad at this particular point. By having Sancho fail to make the obvious distinction between our *dueña* and the *dueña* of romance, Cervantes introduces into his novel a play of opposites. There is not the remotest possibility that any reader could have seen in Doña Rodríguez an allusion to the chivalric *dueña*. By means of the paraphrase Cervantes alludes to the ambiguous duality of *dueña* (role) and *dueña* (contemporary servant) at the very beginning of his treatment of events at the ducal palace, thereby setting the stage for the Trifaldi and Rodríguez episodes through which the theme is to be played out.

Since Doña Rodríguez, a *dueña de servicio* with characteristic faults and defects, is basic to his development of the theme, Cervantes establishes and maintains a connection between her and the already existing stereotype of the *dueña* from the outset. The words that introduce the character link her to the stereotype by association.

> Sancho... se cosió con la duquesa y se entró en el castillo; y remordiéndole la conciencia de que dejaba al jumento solo, se llegó a una reverenda dueña, que con otras a recebir a la duquesa había salido, y con voz baja le dijo:
> —Señora Gonzalez, o cómo es su gracia de vuesa merced...
> —Doña Rodríguez de Grijalba me llamo —respondió la dueña—. ¿Qué es lo que mandáis hermano? (II.31.813).

Sancho addresses the *dueña* as "Señora González" at his first glimpse of her because *González* was a typical surname among *dueñas*.[7] Her

---

age also identifies her with the stereotype, for, like her counterparts in fiction and in reality, Doña Rodríguez is middle-aged. Her advancing age is stressed in Sancho's retort to "... de mí no podréis llevar sino una higa": "¡Aun bien ... que será bien madura, pues no perderá vuesa merced la quínola de sus años por un punto menos!" (31.814). The Duchess' good-natured defense of her *dueña* against Sancho's affronts advances the presentation of Rodríguez as a typical *dueña*:

> —Advertid, Sancho amigo, que doña Rodríguez es muy moza, y que aquellas tocas más la trae por autoridad y por usanza que por los años (31.815).

The *tocas,* a symbol of authority in *dueñas,* as the Duchess explains, are part of the traditional dress of the group, described above in Chapter III. Additionally, Doña Rodríguez wears eyeglasses, a fact we learn during her visit to Don Quijote's chambers (48.939). Poor vision would seem to be an occupational hazard. [8]

Her behavior coincides with the stereotype as well, for she shares in many of the negative qualities that earned the ladies their ill fame in literature and life in the sixteenth and seventeenth centuries. Doña Rodríguez, not Sancho, initiates the quarrelsome tone of their first disagreement. With the bad temper and sharp tongue we spoke of earlier, she says:

> —Si tan discreto es el amo como el mozo ... ¡medradas estamos! Andad hermano, mucho de enhoramala para vos y para quien acá os trujo ... (31.814).

Her language becomes even stronger after Sancho's comment about her age:

> —Hijo de puta ... si soy vieja o no, a Dios daré la cuenta; que no a vos, bellaco, harto de ajos (31.814). [9]

Her outburst is so loud as to call the Duchess' attention to her *dueña,* whom she finds "alborotada" and "encarnizados los ojos" in stark

---

[8] See Chapter III above, note 12.

[9] The language Doña Rodríguez uses is quite strong for a woman who purports to any degree of gentility. Doña Rodríguez claims noble ancestry (48.942).

contrast to the chivalresque demeanor of the other servants. Language of such a nature may very well have given rise to the expression "lo puso cual digan dueñas." [10] Furthermore, the reaction shows Doña Rodríguez is vain, a facet of her character revealed also in her response to Don Quijote's accusation of *tercería*:

> —¿Yo recado de nadie, señor mío? ... aún no estoy en edad tan prolongada que me acoja a semejantes niñerías, pues, Dios loado, mi alma me tengo en las carnes, y todos mis dientes y muelas en la boca, amén de unos pocos que me han usurpado unos catarros, que en esta tierra de Aragón son tan ordinarios (48.940).

While Don Quijote's accusation is of a moral nature, she is so vain as to feel injured only because of the implication of old age. Doña Rodríguez appears more offended by the fact that *terceras* were old women than by their reprehensible actions, which she terms "niñerías." She therefore expends more energy in having it understood that she is not at all elderly than in denying the insulting charge. The attribution of what may be considered a natural consequence of old age (the loss of teeth) to external circumstance, is characteristic of the usual depiction of *dueñas*. [11] Vanity, too, occasions her negative comment on the "negro mongil" worn by *dueñas* — "como quien cubre o tapa un muladar con un tapiz en día de procesión" (37.866). She feels a *dueña*'s good looks may be obscured by the unattractive habit.

Dueñas, as we know, were considered to be talkative and gossips. Once again, Doña Rodríguez' behavior coincides with the stereotype.

---

[10] The expression "cual digan dueñas" is defined in *Dicc. de Aut.* as follows: "Modo de hablar para dar a entender que alguno quedó mal, o fue maltratado, principalmente de palabra." It appears in *Don Quijote* II.8.633 where the knight uses it in an anecdote about a lady who wishes to be included in a famous poet's satire against the ladies of the court: "Hizolo así el poeta, y púsola cual no digan dueñas..." Rodríguez Marín, II.8.152 recalls Cejador's definition: "la trató muy mal de palabra, cual solían las dueñas, ya directamente, ya cuando entre sí charlaban y comentaban los defectos del prójimo." He goes on to note that Quevedo, in using the idiom in "Visita de los chistes," omits the "no" used by Cervantes. Rodríguez Marín does not explain the discrepancy. It might be that Cervantes uses the negative as an intensifier, to mean "la puso cual [aún] no dirían dueñas."

[11] Cervantes uses the same technique in showing the vanity of the *dueña* of *La casa de los celos*, who claims that the condition of her complexion is caused by the climate of France (see Chapter III above). See also Clemencín's note on this same subject, II.48.457.

As proof of her talkativeness, we may point to the *dueña*'s interruption of conversations that do not at all concern her. She interjects foolish comment into Sancho's conversation with the Duchess (33.838) and interrupts him in the "coloquio dueñesco" with a defense of *dueñas* as a class (37.866). She is so verbose as to relate at length her late husband's story to Don Quijote, despite having just claimed "que no tenía lugar para contarle" and the fact that there are more important matters to be discussed (48.943). Her ensuing revelations to Don Quijote about Altisidora's bad breath and the Duchess' issues (*fuentes*) are pure gossip (48.945). [12] She is punished for these particular negative qualities through the beating she receives from the eavesdropping Duchess and Altisidora. With considerable cause she also discloses to the *hidalgo* the Duke's indebtedness to a rich farmer. Although *dueñas* were known as *terceras* in contemporary literature, Doña Rodríguez is not in any way an intermediary or a go-between. However, Don Quijote does suspect her of it. More will be said of this later.

The many negative comments made about *dueñas* in Part II further reinforce the identification of Rodríguez with the stereotype of the *dueña de servicio* as a troublesome servant. [13] Relating his altercation with the *dueña* to the Duchess, Sancho states:

---

[12] Arco, *Sociedad*, 406-407 indicates that these ulcerations became almost fashionable in the seventeenth century, and that they were not at all unusual after about 1657. It was thought they were beneficial to health and beauty. We may conclude that the Duchess' *fuentes* might have been occasioned as much by vanity as by medical necessity.

[13] While most of the comments are made by Sancho and Don Quijote, Cervantes criticizes *dueñas* directly as narrator, through Cide Hamete. Explaining how the Duchess and Altisidora came to be informed of Doña Rodríguez' presence in Don Quijote's chambers, he writes:

> "Dice Cide Hamete, puntualísimo escudriñador de los átomos desta verdadera historia, que al tiempo que doña Rodríguez salió de su aposento para ir a la estancia de don Quijote, otra dueña que con ella dormía lo sintió, y que *como todas las dueñas son amigas de saber, entender y oler*, se fue tras ella, con tanto silencio, que la buena Rodríguez no lo echó de ver; y así como la dueña la vio entrar en la estancia de don Quijote, porque no faltase en ella *la general costumbre que todas las dueñas tienen de ser chismosas*, al momento lo fue a poner en pico a su señora la duquesa, de cómo doña Rodríguez quedaba en el aposento de don Quijote" (50.958).

This particular *dueña* is the only other *dueña* of the Duchess' service singled out for individual treatment by Cervantes. Significantly, it is the stereotype he refers to. This *dueña* is nosy, a gossip and a troublemaker.

> ...A esta señora le rogué... tuviese cuenta con él [mi asno], y azoróse de manera como si la hubiera dicho que era fea o vieja, debiendo ser más propio y natural de las dueñas pensar jumentos que autorizar las salas. ¡Oh, válame Dios, y cuán mal estaba con estas señoras un hidalgo de mi lugar! (33.841-842).

For Sancho, Doña Rodríguez is a typical *dueña* — the kind disliked by an "hidalgo de mi lugar." In his opinion, Rodríguez and her ilk are better suited for chores in the stable than for their assigned tasks in the home. He attributes similar sentiments to a "boticario toledano" in the "coloquio dueñesco," saying, in relation to Trifaldi's arrival:

> ...Yo he oído decir a un boticario toledano que hablaba como un silguero que donde interviniesen dueñas no podía suceder cosa buena. ¡Válame Dios, y qué mal estaba con ellas el tal boticario! De lo que yo saco que... todas las dueñas son enfadosas e impertinentes... (37.865).

As in the statement above, Sancho's simulated citation of an "authority" is intended to lend weight to his own opinion. Elements of both statements are formulaic: "¡Válame Dios, y cuán/qué mal estaba...!" Sancho shares the popular belief that all *dueñas* are troublesome, and thus he holds that any *dueña* — Rodríguez or Trifaldi — will be.

Through both these passages, moreover, Cervantes alludes once more to the ambiguity of *dueña/dueña de servicio*. In the first case, Sancho expresses his disdain for contemporary *dueñas* such as Doña Rodríguez in a context that calls to mind his recital of the ballad with its reference to chivalric *dueñas*. In the second, he voices his dislike for the figures of contemporary society at the time when the announcement of the arrival of the chivalric *dueña* Trifaldi has been made. Although Don Quijote's clarification of the matter — "esta señora dueña... no debe ser de aquellas que el boticario toledano tiene en su número..." — alludes to the distinction that is to be made between these disparate kinds of *dueñas,* Sancho and Doña Rodríguez continue to argue over the merits or demerits of *dueñas,* unaware that there is any difference at all from the literary role to the contemporary servant. It is part of the underlying conceit that when Trifaldi appears, the two *dueñas,* never before juxtaposed, much less merged, are blended together, as the *mayordomo* infuses the defects of the servant into his depiction of the role of the *dueña* of romance.

Don Quijote's negative views on *dueñas,* also directly related to Doña Rodríguez, are all the more striking because of his initial defense of the *dueña* against Sancho: "Dime, truhán moderno y majadero antiguo: ¿parécete bien deshonrar y afrentar a una dueña tan veneranda y digna de respeto como aquélla?" (42.816). The knight's feelings with respect to *dueñas* become evident during her visit to his chambers, and his observations at this point are a withering attack on *dueñas* as a class as well as on Rodríguez herself. Having accepted her denial of "tercería," he next accuses her of lasciviousness. In a clear allusion to the sensual inclination of *dueñas,* he suspects Doña Rodríguez of being a tool of the devil, sent to tempt him:

> —¿Quién sabe si el diablo, que es sutil y mañoso, querrá engañarme agora con una dueña, lo que no ha podido con emperatrices, reinas, duquesas, marquesas ni condesas? Que yo he oído decir muchas veces ... que, si él puede, antes os la dará roma que aguileña. Y ¿quién sabe si esta soledad, esta ocasión y este silencio despertará mis deseos que duermen, y harán que al cabo de mis años venga a caer donde nunca he tropezado? (48.940). [14]

Don Quijote, aware of the distinction between the *dueña* of romance and the contemporary servant, attributes to her the defects of the group. His reasons for rejecting his fears as ludicrous further denigrate *dueñas:*

> Pero yo no debo de estar en mi juicio, pues tales disparates digo y pienso, que no es posible que una dueña toquiblanca, larga y antojuna pueda mover ni levantar pensamiento lascivo en el más desalmado pecho del mundo. ¿Por ventura hay dueña en la tierra que tenga buenas carnes? ¿Por ventura hay dueña en el orbe que deje de ser impertinente, fruncida y melindrosa? ¡Afuera, pues, caterva dueñesca, inútil para

---

[14] It will be remembered that Rodríguez Marín, "Las dueñas," *Don Quijote,* X, p. 65, claims that sermons of the times contained the allegation that the devil led women astray with *dueñas.* There is also a literary precedent. In the *Caballero Cifar* the devil takes the form of a beautiful *dueña* (lady) on three occasions to tempt Roboan (pp. 461, 464 and 471). The same *"dueña"* appears later to Roboan and the Emperor of Trigrida to mock them for having heeded her advice (p. 483). See María Rosa Lida de Malkiel, "La visión de trasmundo en las literaturas hispánicas," in *El otro mundo en la literatura medieval*..., Howard Rollin Patch (Mexico, 1956), pp. 410-412 and pp. 413-414.

ningún humano regalo! ¡Oh cuán bien hacía aquella señora de quien se dice que tenía dos dueñas de bulto con sus antojos y almohadillas al cabo de su estrado, como que estaban labrando, y tanto le servían para la autoridad de su sala aquellas estatuas como las dueñas verdaderas! (48.941).

Don Quijote has progressed from a specific condemnation of Rodríguez to a condemnation of *dueñas* as a class. He attacks their morals, appearance, behavior and social usefulness. Clearly, Sancho and Don Quijote's opinions reflect Cervantes' own. These passages, together with the attacks on *dueñas* in *El licenciado Vidriera* and *El celoso extremeño,* constitute the most complete and all-inclusive denunciation of the *dueña* by any sixteenth- or seventeenth-century author that has come to my attention.

Other details complete the identification of Doña Rodríguez with the stereotype. The feud between *dueñas* and *escuderos,* embodied in the numerous disputes between Sancho and Rodríguez, may reflect contemporary reality. [15] Doña Rodríguez says:

> —Siempre los escuderos... son enemigos nuestros; que como son duendes de las antesalas y nos veen a cada paso, los ratos que no rezan, que son muchos, los gastan en murmurar de nosotras, desterrándonos los huesos y enterrándonos la fama (37.866).

The feud between Sancho, squire, and Doña Rodríguez, *dueña,* begins in their first meeting, when they argue over the stabling of his ass, and continues in all the "coloquio dueñesco." Cervantes portrays Doña Rodríguez' attitude toward *escuderos* as that of the typical *dueña.* Likewise, Sancho's reaction to Trifaldi may be viewed within the context of this animosity, as may his protestations at being pinched by *dueñas* in his second stay at the ducal palace (69.1105-1106). [16] He

---

[15] Clemencín, II.31.128 observed "Los escuderos y las dueñas solían ordinariamente ser antagonistas... Dueñas y escuderos eran personas poco ocupadas, y servían más para la autoridad de las casas que para la comodidad de sus dueños: los unos y las otras eran gente de edad madura, y el coco de la juventud que solía vengarse con ridicularizarlos."

[16] At that point he strongly objects to being touched by *dueñas,* and complains their hands smell of vinegar lotion (69.1106). Riquer, in a footnote, explains that *vinagrillo* was a cosmetic used to whiten face and hands. See also Arco, *Sociedad,* 402. Once again, in dealing with *dueñas,* Cervantes alludes to a defect of the class — vanity.

has assumed the role of antagonist to *dueñas* — the role of the contemporary *escudero*.

We have outlined briefly here Doña Rodríguez' relation to the stereotype. In his treatment of the *dueña* as such Cervantes accorded the figure the most extensive attention given her in literature to that date, and, had he intended to pursue the theme no further in *Don Quijote* II, his development of *dueñas* would still have had literary significance. However, the basic conceit of the duality *dueña/dueña de servicio* lay beneath the surface of the entire development from the time Sancho quoted the ballad. Although Cervantes systematically presented Rodríguez as a *dueña de servicio,* a type easily recognizable to his contemporary readers, he alluded to the underlying ambiguity of *dueña/dueña de servicio* at three points in the text: 1) at the time of Rodríguez' introduction as a character during the arrival at the palace, 2) shortly thereafter in reinforcement (II.33.841) and 3) when Trifaldi was introduced. From this conceit, Cervantes now advances to a more meaningful and subtle treatment of Doña Rodríguez as part of major themes related to the novel as a whole.

His treatment of the theme of *dueñas* and *doncellas,* presented in Chapter IV above, is concomitant to his development of the theme of *dueñas* in the Doña Rodríguez episode, Chapters 48 and 52. It is our intention to show the significance of Doña Rodríguez' reenactment of the role of *dueña menesterosa.* For reasons that will become evident later, it is important that she carry out the role as a full character. In contradiction to her complete identification with the stereotype, Doña Rodríguez is neither a type nor a caricature. [17] While Cervantes depicts Rodríguez as a typical *dueña,* he begins simultaneously to develop her as a character in her own right, with individual foibles and traits, and with a personal life unrelated to the stereotype.

Our *dueña* is too naive and simpleminded to be typical, as her reaction to Sancho's paraphrase of "Lanzarote" attests. She fails to recognize the highly popular ballad, or even, it would seem, that the words are in verse form. She is unfamiliar with the name 'Lanzarote,' whom she assumes to be a real individual, and fails to recognize the geographic name 'Bretaña.' Explaining her anger to the Duchess, she says:

---

[17] Casalduero, *Sentido,* 213. He interprets Doña Rodríguez as a caricature.

—Aquí las he... con este buen hombre, que me ha
pedido encarecidamente que vaya a poner en la caballeriza
a un asno suyo que está a la puerta del castillo, trayéndome
por ejemplo que así lo hicieron no sé dónde, que unas damas
curaron a un tal Lanzarote, y unas dueñas a su rocino...
(31.814-815).

Her words in addition suggest that she has not grasped "curar de"
in its old acceptation of "cuidar," "to attend to," confusing it with
"curar a," "to cure." Cervantes contrasts the reality of the *dueña*'s
stupidity and evident ignorance with the stylized *dueña* of fiction,
and it is part of the conceit that she should have no knowledge at all
of the situation and figures whose example has so enraged her.

Her comments on Sancho's reference to the ballad of "La penitencia del rey don Rodrigo" are another index of her ingenuousness.
In her foolishness she accepts the ballad's content as undisputed
historical fact.

—Y ¡cómo que no mienten [las trovas de los romances
antiguos]!... que un romance hay que dice que metieron
al rey Rodrigo, vivo vivo, en una tumba llena de sapos,
culebras y lagartos, y que de allí a dos días dijo el rey desde
dentro de la tumba, con voz doliente y baja:

ya me comen, ya me comen
por do más pecado había;

y según esto, mucha razón tiene este señor en decir que
quiere más ser más labrador que rey, si le han de comer
sabandijas (33.838).

Cervantes stresses Rodríguez' naiveté by means of the Duchess'
reaction: "No pudo la duquesa tener la risa oyendo la simplicidad
de su dueña" (33.838). It may be noted that the *dueña* takes the idea
of Sancho's proposed governorship, the topic of the conversation at
the point she interrupts, seriously. It is doubtful that an individual of
average intelligence would have done so. Thus Cervantes establishes
rank credulity and naiveté as Doña Rodríguez' dominant traits. These
traits are important, for her subsequent actions follow directly from
her character, which is given definitive form in the scene of her
nocturnal visit to Don Quijote's chambers (Chapter 48). However,
before proceeding, it would be well to deal with the literary basis of
the chapter.

On one level Chapter 48 parodies the chivalric commonplace we have spoken of so often — the nocturnal visit of an enamored noble damsel to the palace chambers of a visiting knight. In 1605 Cervantes parodied the motif as part of the theme of *doncellas* (Chapter IV above). There are substantial differences. If, in 1605, Don Quijote was kept awake because of his eager anticipation of the imagined visit of the daughter of the lord of the castle (I.16.159), in 1615 sadness and melancholy, occasioned by his misfortunes and Altisidora's romantic persecutions, disturb his sleep. Where once the image of his lady could protect him from the onslaught of even Guinevere and Quintañona, her image now is more a cause for sorrow than for inspiration. His pride, too, has been hurt by the results of his attempt to soothe the "unhappiness" of the *doncella* Altisidora, that concluded with the painful battle of the cats.

In II.48 his evocation of the theme upon hearing the key turn in the lock of his room is justified, for Altisidora, in her burlesque imitation of an enamored damsel, has led him to believe she is in love with him. Don Quijote expects the nocturnal visit because it is in keeping with the traditional development of the love between knight and damsel in the prose romances. The parody is seen immediately. Even while pledging fidelity to his lady, Don Quijote cannot forget that Dulcinea has been transformed into a "cebolluda labradora" (938). He cannot imagine her as if she were a noblewoman like Guinevere or Oriana, for he now remembers her as a mere peasant. Further, Don Quijote is not a young Perión or Galaz, but a completely anti-chivalric figure, a fact underlined by Cervantes' description of the knight:

> Púsose en pie sobre la cama, envuelto de arriba abajo en una colcha de raso amarillo, una galocha en la cabeza, y el rostro y los bigotes vendados: el rostro por los arruños; los bigotes, porque no se le desmayasen y cayesen, en el cual traje parecía la más extraordinaria fantasma que se pudiera pensar (48.938).

Doña Rodríguez is not a beautiful, young damsel, but a middle-aged "reverendísima dueña," with an unusually long white headdress and huge eyeglasses, an exaggeration of the dress of *dueñas* that makes her true identity all too obvious:

> [Don Quijote] Clavó los ojos en la puerta, y cuando es-
> peraba ver entrar por ella a la rendida y lastimada Altisidora,
> vio entrar a una reverendísima dueña con unas tocas blancas
> repulgadas y luengas, tanto, que la cubrían y enmantaban
> desde los pies a la cabeza. Entre los dedos de la mano iz-
> quierda traía una media vela encendida, y con la derecha se
> hacía sombra, porque no le diese la luz en los ojos, a quien
> cubrían unos muy grandes antojos. Venía pisando quedito, y
> movía los pies blandamente (48.938-939).

She becomes so frightened upon seeing him — "¡Jesús! ¿Qué es lo
que veo?" — that, in trying to flee, entangled in her skirts, "dio
consigo una gran caída" (939). Likewise, Don Quijote now believes
the white vision before him is a witch, a ghost or a condemned soul.
Cervantes adds "... Si él quedó medroso en ver tal figura, ella quedó
espantada en ver la suya..." (939). He parodies the literary motif
by way of the identity, age and physical condition of the two protagonists.

Cervantes' emphasis on the characters in II.48 represents an advance over his treatment of the same motif in I.16, where the parody
depended in part on coincidence and circumstance. Maritornes, for
instance, was on her way to join her muleteer when she met with
Don Quijote. Moreover, in 1615 he raises the parody of chivalric
themes to a more complex level. Doña Rodríguez, sufficiently re-
covered from her fright to identify herself, explains:

> Señor don Quijote, si es que acaso vuestra merced es
> don Quijote, yo no soy fantasma, ni visión, ni alma de pur-
> gatorio... sino doña Rodríguez, la dueña de honor de mi
> señora la duquesa, que con una necesidad de aquellas que
> vuestra merced suele remediar, a vuestra merced vengo
> (48.939).

Cervantes begins with a parody of the damsel's visit to her knight's
chambers; but, since the visit is carried out by a *dueña* with a *cuita*,
he is also alluding to the theme of the *dueña menesterosa*. Furthermore, the *dueña* in question is a contemporary *dueña de servicio*.
There are many elements in the episode that we need to study point
by point.

Firstly, Don Quijote does not recognize the situation of *dueña
menesterosa* (*dueña*-in-distress) seeking a knight's aid. Now that a
legitimate chivalric adventure presents itself to our knight, he fails to

grasp the significance. Why is this? Doña Rodríguez has unwittingly used the structure of one chivalric motif (nocturnal visit of damsel to knight) to carry out another one (*dueña*-in-distress). Cervantes' wit determines that although our *dueña*'s intentions in her nocturnal visit were to seek aid, the manner of her coming clearly parallels the first theme. [18] Don Quijote perceives only the outward appearances of the encounter. Moreover, seeing a *dueña* before him, he takes her to be a go-between. He says:

> ... ¿por ventura viene vuestra merced a hacer alguna tercería? Porque le hago saber que yo no soy de provecho para nadie, merced a la sin par belleza de mi señora Dulcinea del Toboso. Digo, en fin, señora doña Rodríguez, que como vuestra merced salve y deje a una parte todo recado amoroso, puede volver a encender su vela, y vuelva, y departiremos de todo lo que más mandare y más en gusto le viniere, salvo, como digo, todo incitativo melindre (940).

On the occasions in Part I when Don Quijote either evoked the image of an intermediary *dueña* (Quintañona in I.16) or perceived a woman as a *dueña* (Maritornes in I.43), it was in the context of "honrada dueña" or "discreta dueña." For Don Quijote Quintañona and chivalric *dueñas* of her kind represented great ladies with a noble mission on behalf of ladies of high rank. In I.43 Don Quijote treated the "intermediary *dueña*" Maritornes with respect. How then are we to explain his attitude toward Doña Rodríguez in 1615? Only her speedy return to his room after lighting her candle prevents his locking the door against her. As the tirade against *dueñas* (939-940) reveals, Don Quijote correctly identified Rodríguez as the contemporary servant she is, and the realization immediately destroyed his earlier evocation of the chivalric motif. The image of the contemporary *dueña* was that of a go-between of questionable integrity and of lascivious inclinations, and she merited no special respect or consideration. [19] If the *dueña*

---

[18] One of the factors responsible for the confusion in themes is that the *dueña* should call upon Don Quijote at night. There are two possible explanations for her choice of time. First, it is logical that she should wish to speak to Don Quijote about her personal problems in private. Her own day-time attendance upon the Duchess would give her little opportunity to do so. Secondly, the idea of a nocturnal visit may have been suggested to her by Altisidora's night-time pursuance of Don Quijote (Chapters 44 and 46).

[19] For Don Quijote's statements see above, pp. 120-121.

who has come to his room at such an hour was not acting in behalf of another, then she must have come in pursuit of her own base desires. Significantly, Don Quijote changes his direct address of the *dueña* from "vuestra merced" to "vos" after she reenters his room (48.941). Although the Duchess presents her servants to Don Quijote as the *dueñas* and *doncellas* of chivalric romance, it is unthinkable for Don Quijote to see in a *dueña de servicio*, with *antojos* and *tocas*, the *dueña* of chivalric romance. Here he sees the difference and would not take the one as the other.

Cervantes' emphasis on the individuality and personality of the two characters moves the episode away from mere parody or caricature. He shows Doña Rodríguez at variance with the stereotype of the *dueña* brought up by Don Quijote during her absence from the room, and suggested by her own dress and manner. She is seen to be, rather, a foolish and vain older woman afraid of being violated despite her age and appearance, and the evident physical condition of Don Quijote. Backing away from him in fear, she says "¿Estamos seguras, señor caballero? porque no tengo a muy honesta señal haberse vuesa merced levantado de su lecho" (941). Similarly, Don Quijote is afraid of being "acometido y forzado," for he is not made of marble, nor she of bronze, and because it is late, and they are "en una estancia más cerrada y secreta que lo debió de ser la cueva donde el traidor Eneas gozó a la hermosa y piadosa Dido" (941).[20] The fears of the two characters individualize them. They interact as people, foolish as they may be, not as types.

The details of her life which Doña Rodríguez recounts to Don Quijote further individualize her, and serve, in part, to explain her foolish nature. Who is Doña Rodríguez, and how did she become a *dueña*? We learn that she was born in Asturias. Her impoverished parents took her to Madrid as a young woman so that she could enter into the service of a lady of some importance as a *doncella de labor*. Orphaned within a few years, she depended entirely upon her salary for subsistence. She married an older man, a simpleminded *escudero*, who was eventually fired. Soon widowed, she again finds herself alone

---

[20] Don Quijote's rather comical comparison of himself to Aeneas (by allusion) could have been suggested to him by Altisidora. When the *doncella* sang beneath his window she called him a "nuevo Eneas" (44.912). Don Quijote is sufficiently impressionable to accept the idea.

and unprotected, with the additional responsibility of a child. At this point, she passes into the service of the Duchess, who hires her because of her fame with the needle. Doña Rodríguez' story is such that we cannot expect great perspicacity from her. Given the circumstances, she has done her best. Undeniably, her story in part coincides with that of the typical *dueña*: a widow forced into service through poverty. Humorous personal details continue to emphasize the individual woman as opposed to the typical *dueña*. For instance, she sees her husband's stupidity as good breeding and courtesy. His inappropriate insistence on accompanying an "alcalde de corte," while leading his lady's mount, resulted in her falling from the mule and his subsequent dismissal. But Rodríguez explains:

> Divulgóse la cortesía de mi esposo, tanto, que los muchachos le corrían por las calles, y por esto y porque él era algún tanto corto de vista, mi señora la duquesa le despidió, de cuyo pesar, sin duda alguna, tengo para mí que se le causó el mal de la muerte (48.943-944).

In addition, as any proud mother, she praises her daughter at length:

> ... Creció mi hija, y con ella todo el donaire del mundo: canta como una calandria, danza como el pensamiento, baila como una perdida, lee y escribe como un maestro de escuela, y cuenta como un avariento. De su limpieza no digo nada: que el agua que corre no es más limpia, y debe de tener agora, si mal no me acuerdo, diez y seis años, cinco meses y tres días, uno más a menos (944).

The jarring comparisons and statements ("cuenta como un avariento"), of course, are consistent with her personality. Doña Rodríguez, as a widow and a mother, whose main concern is the welfare of her daughter, is no longer just a *dueña*, but a full character as well.

Because the Doña Rodríguez episode provides some of the most comic moments of *Don Quijote*, the comicity may divert our attention from the episode's originality and importance. At no other point in the novel does a real person, filled with anxiety, bring a real, contemporary problem for Don Quijote to solve as a knight in the manner of the romances. Don Quijote's handling of the matter relates directly to two major themes of the novel: Don Quijote's ineffectuality and the theme of literature and life. Cervantes connects the Doña Rodríguez episode to these underlying themes.

Doña Rodríguez recurs to Don Quijote so that he may remedy a wrong done to her daughter. The novelty of Cervantes' treatment of the theme of *dueña*-in-distress is evident: the great lady of the romances has been reduced to a *dueña de servicio*. Transferring the situation of *dueña*-in-distress seeking out a knight to the sixteenth century, we find that the only kind of *dueña* existing at that time is a mere *dueña de servicio,* and the only knight from whom she can seek redress is but a mock-knight. Cervantes merges two themes, one traditional and one contemporary, and proceeds from this point. The *dueña*'s *cuita* consists not in the usurpation of her lands, nor in the abduction of a noble husband or daughter (chivalric convention), but in the seduction and abandonment of her daughter. Although many *dueñas* were accused of *tercería,* in this case we find a kind of reversal, in that it is a *dueña*'s daughter, not a charge, who is seduced. Doña Rodríguez explains:

> ... Desta mi muchacha se enamoró un hijo de un labra-
> dor riquísimo que está en una aldea del duque mi señor ...
> En efecto, no sé cómo ni cómo no, ellos se juntaron, y debajo
> de la palabra de ser su esposo, burló a mi hija, y no se la
> quiere cumplir ... (944).

Our knight is asked to obligate the young man to keep his word. Doña Rodríguez' problem is real and contemporary, unrelated to the ideal world of chivalric romance.

What concurrence of events could have driven Doña Rodríguez to attempt to solve her problem in such a way: to accept Don Quijote as a real knight-errant and to have recourse to his aid, thereby assuming a literary role? We can state from the outset that Doña Rodríguez, unlike the other servants of the ducal palace, is not aware that she is imitating the art of the prose romances. It is implausible that a woman who is barely aware of the ballads should have sufficient knowledge of the romances to do so. We will find her motivation — her daughter's seduction — in life, not in literature. But literature, indirectly, provides the mode. It is evident that the Trifaldi episode has influenced Doña Rodríguez' decision to seek Don Quijote's help. The *dueña*'s actions are in character. We know that, because of her credulity and simplemindedness, she confuses fiction with reality. More exactly, she fails to recognize fiction when it confronts her ("Lanzarote") and also accepts legend as truth ("La penitencia del rey don Rodrigo"). It is therefore consistent with her character that she should have accepted Don Quijote as a real knight-errant. She has seen everyone treat him as if he were, from the moment he arrived at the palace. Events in the ducal palace mislead her. It is also natural that she should have been deceived by the Trifaldi hoax, where she witnessed a *dueña* with a problem not unlike her own seek and receive Don Quijote's assistance. To have penetrated the mock nature of the Trifaldi affair it would have been necessary to be familiar with the romances, to realize they were fiction, to have understood the character and intent of the Duke and Duchess, and, at the very least, to be endowed with some measure of common sense. Doña Rodríguez, the antithesis of the *mayordomo,* has neither the psychological nor the literary understanding to comprehend the incident. It will be remembered that not all spectators were informed, and that Sancho also, despite the unbelievable beards, was taken in.

We may ask ourselves why the Trifaldi affair so impressed Doña Rodríguez as to influence her behavior. First, after the squire Trifaldín's speech, in keeping with the format of the romances, Don Quijote formulates a definition of knights-errant that is important for the *dueña.*

> ... Los extraordinariamente afligidos y desconsolados, en casos grandes y en desdichas inormes no van a buscar su remedio a las casas de los letrados, ... ni al caballero que nunca ha acertado a salir de los términos de su lugar, ni al perezoso cortesano ... el remedio de las cuitas, el socorro de las necesidades, el amparo de las doncellas, el consuelo de las viudas, en ninguna suerte de personas se halla mejor que en los caballeros andantes, y de serlo yo doy infinitas gracias al cielo ... venga esta dueña, y pida lo que quisiere; que yo le libraré su remedio en la fuerza de mi brazo y en la intrépida resolución de mi animoso espíritu (37.864-865).

The words are apt to Doña Rodríguez' situation. She is a widow who needs "consuelo" in a "desdicha inorme." Her daughter is a "doncella" who needs "amparo." Doña Rodríguez can easily count herself among those ladies whom knights are honor-bound to aid. In addition, the Trifaldi affair concerns a *dueña* with a *cuita.* We have already stated that Doña Rodríguez does not understand she and Trifaldi are different kinds of *dueñas.* She associates Trifaldi with the contemporary *dueña.* The "coloquio dueñesco" shows she identifies with Trifaldi. Her comment "Dueñas tiene mi señora la duquesa en su servicio que pudieran ser condesas si la fortuna quisiera" (37.866) is telling. For Doña Rodríguez a mere caprice of fortune separates her from Trifaldi's apparent status and prestige. The possessive adjective of "siempre los escuderos son enemigos nuestros" had already shown her in the process of identifying herself with Trifaldi.

The substance of Trifaldi's complaint is also decisive in influencing Doña Rodríguez. There are parallels between the feigned problem of the Dolorida and the real one of our *dueña*. In her story, the Countess claims that her charge, Antonomasia, was seduced by a young man, Clavijo, "debajo del título de verdadero esposo" (39.874). There is social inequality between the lovers: princess, knight. It immediately comes to mind that the problem of Doña Rodríguez' daughter is similar. Rodríguez' daughter was seduced by the son of a rich farmer "debajo de palabra de ser su esposo" (48.944). There is also social inequality between the lovers, although in reverse: attendant, farmer's son. It is not a question of narrative symmetry. Rather, the Trifaldi affair influences Rodríguez. Even she could not have failed to see the parallel in the two situations. If Don Quijote was able to resolve Trifaldi's problem, why then could he not resolve hers? The *dueña* can seek redress from no one else. She explains to Don Quijote that although she had sought the Duke's aid on many occasions, he refused to intervene in the matter for personal reasons. [21]

The facts of the Trifaldi episode deceive Doña Rodríguez. Ingenuous and foolish, she has believed everything she has seen and heard in the ducal palace since Don Quijote's arrival. Cervantes shows this most clearly. Upon entering Don Quijote's chambers she had explained: "... yo no soy... sino doña Rodríguez... *que con una necesidad de aquellas que vuestra merced suele remediar, a vuestra merced vengo*" (48.939). Having finished her story, she adds:

> Querría, pues, señor mío, que vuesa merced tomase a cargo el deshacer este agravio, o ya por ruegos, o ya por armas, *pues según todo el mundo dice, vuesa merced nació en él para deshacerlos, y para enderezar los tuertos y amparar los miserables* ... (48.944).

---

[21] It will be remembered that the Dueña de Noruega seeks Agrajes out under similar circumstances. Her own ruler cannot give her justice, and she must seek the solution to the *cuita* elsewhere.

In no way conscious of playing a literary role, she seeks out Don Quijote, misled by trickery, and her own desperation and foolishness.

The episodes dealing with Doña Rodríguez and the Dueña Dolorida contrast with one another. The Dolorida is a false *dueña* with a fictitious problem, and the episode constitutes a hoax perpetrated upon Don Quijote. Doña Rodríguez, on the other hand, is a real *dueña* of contemporary society, with a real problem. Trifaldi — Art — more than prefigures Rodríguez — Life. While mockery, make-believe does, in a way, turn into life, Cervantes carries the idea farther. Joaquín Casalduero touches upon the problem when he states "En 1605 la experiencia vital se transforma en arte — Dorotea en Princesa Micomicona —, en 1615 el arte ilumina la vida — dueña Dolorida, doña Rodríguez." [22] More precisely, in 1615 art can lead to deception and error in real life, with grave consequences for the deceived. Doña Rodríguez, unlike Don Quijote, is not moved to relive the romances. But she tries to solve a real problem with an unwitting imitation of their art. In 1615 Cervantes explores the consequences of the confusion of life and literature by a real individual. It is for this reason that we emphasized earlier the importance of Doña Rodríguez' reenactment of the role of *dueña menesterosa* as a full character — an individual — rather than as a type.

Having presented her problem to Don Quijote once, our *dueña* is driven to an even more direct imitation of the Trifaldi episode. She has persisted in her design despite the beating she received at the close of Chapter 48. The title of Chapter 52 announces that Doña Rodríguez will take the role of the "segunda dueña Dolorida." Mother and daughter present themselves in the main salon of the palace, dressed in mourning, to ask Don Quijote in all formality to right the wrong. Cervantes leads his readers to expect an even more obvious parody of the theme of *dueña*-in-distress. Doña Rodríguez is to imitate the format of the Trifaldi episode to the best of her ability.

Before turning to the episode, we must ask ourselves why Doña Rodríguez should attempt a second meeting, and so formal and public a one, with Don Quijote. In II.48 Don Quijote has only casually promised to help her. His words do not constitute a vow to undertake her cause. Before she relates her tale, he says only:

---

[22] Casalduero, *Sentido*, 229.

—Puede vuesa merced... desbuchar todo aquello que
tiene dentro de su cuitado corazón y lastimadas entrañas,
que será de mí escuchada con castos oídos, y socorrida con
piadosas obras (48.942).

The consequences of her *dueña*'s gossip bring the meeting to an
abrupt end before Don Quijote can make a definitive statement of
willingness to undertake the adventure. Doña Rodríguez cannot be
sure of Don Quijote's intentions. These indeed are rather ambiguous.
At one point he does seem to have in mind undertaking the cause, as
his letter to Sancho shows:

Un negocio se me ha ofrecido, que creo que me ha de
poner en desgracia destos señores; pero aunque se me da
mucho, no se me da nada, pues, en fin en fin, tengo de cum-
plir antes con mi profesión que con su gusto... (51.973).

Don Quijote's words indicate he is not eager to comply with the
dueña's request. He seems to consider the task a duty he must fulfill,
and, at best, he is unenthusiastic. Hence, it is not surprising that he
appears to forget the incident entirely. Once recuperated from his
painful nocturnal encounters, he plans to leave the ducal palace
(52.976-977). Left to his own devices, he would have failed to undertake the one adventure of his career presented to him, in good
faith, as knight-errant.

Doña Rodríguez' words in her second encounter with Don Quijote
indicate she has been induced to come before him a second time,
because she believes he is leaving without attending to her problem.
She says:

Días ha, valeroso caballero, que os tengo dada cuenta de
la sinrazón y alevosía que un mal labrador tiene fecha a mi
muy querida y amada fija... y vos me habedes prometido
de volver por ella, enderezándole el tuerto que le tienen
fecho, y agora ha llegado a mi noticia que os queredes partir
deste castillo... y así, querría que antes que os escurriésedes
por esos caminos, desafiásedes a este rústico indómito, y le
hicésedes que se casase con mi hija... (52.977).

The *dueña* seems to believe that a formal and public presentation of
her case to the knight will bring about the desired results. Her
imitation of the Trifaldi episode is quite accurate. Behind her sim-

plemindedness we perceive Cervantes' ingenuity and wit. Like Trifaldi (862) she brings her request to Don Quijote after dinner (977). Following the typical features of the *dueña*-in-distress motif, as demonstrated both in the romances and in the Trifaldi episode (where she observed them), the *dueña* is dressed in black. [23] She casts herself at the knight's feet, and shows outward signs of her affliction as she weeps and sighs. Cervantes' description follows:

> Y estando un día a la mesa con los duques, . . . veis aquí a deshora entrar por la puerta de la gran sala dos mujeres, como después pareció, cubiertas de luto de los pies a la cabeza, y la una dellas, llegándose a don Quijote, se le echó a los pies tendida de largo a largo, la boca cosida con los pies de don Quijote, y daba unos gemidos tan tristes, tan profundos y tan dolorosos, que puso en confusión a todos los que la oían y miraban . . . (52.977).

We have the formal presentation of the *cuita* (above), and the formal acceptance of the undertaking: "Yo tomo a mi cargo el remedio de vuestra hija" (978). Doña Rodríguez even attempts to use archaic language, but is unable to sustain it to the end, where 'fija' reverts to 'hija.'

The imitation of Trifaldi carried out by Rodríguez comes closer to the situation of the romances than does the model itself. The very pomp found in Trifaldi's entrance into the palace was atypical. Doña Rodríguez' imitation, necessarily more simple, reproduces in form the development of the situation in the romances. The Trifaldi episode was intended as a mock, and the parody was partly brought about by the ridiculous aspects of the depiction: the large entourage, the manner of telling the story, its content and the beards. On the whole, however, there is little difference in form between the fiction of the Trifaldi episode and the truth of the Rodríguez episode, and the greatest difference lies in the substance. Doña Rodríguez is in earnest. The reaction of the listeners emphasizes the point. The Trifaldi

---

[23] Clemencín, II.52.66 points out "Los ejemplos de dueñas vestidas en paños negros que en este traje se presentan a pedir a los caballeros andantes el favor y ayuda son frecuentes en los libros de caballerías. Imitólas, o por mejor decir, ridiculizólas Cervantes en este caso y en el de la condesa Trifaldi. Por lo demás, se guardan los usos caballerescos." We studied the format in Chapter II. It can be seen that Cervantes does indeed follow the outlines and distinguishing features of such encounters.

episode, pure entertainment, causes laughter, amusement and appreciation for its ingenuity, as was intended. No one laughs during Doña Rodríguez' presentation of her complaint. The reaction, on the contrary, is confusion, wonderment and amazement (977). The Duke and Duchess, even expecting another "burla" planned for their entertainment by their servants, are "dudosos y suspensos." Although Doña Rodríguez may be playing a role in her folly, her unhappiness is real, and with just cause. When the *dueña* identifies herself, betraying her simplemindedness in full view of the public, everyone is astonished: "Admiráronse todos aquellos que la conocían, y más los duques que ninguno; que puesto que la tenían por boba y de buen pasta, no por tanto, que viniese a hacer locuras" (977). To undertake to solve life's injustices through an imitation of fiction is madness.

Cervantes directs the second presentation of the *cuita* toward a specific end. The Doña Rodríguez episode is exemplary, and part of the exemplarity of *Don Quijote* I and II. In an attempt to control the situation for his own amusement and to punish Doña Rodríguez' temerity, the Duke arranges a "duel," in which his lackey Tosilos is to play the part of the young seducer, who in the meantime has run off to Flanders. The duel is to follow chivalric usage scrupulously. Tosilos is coached in detail (54.990) so that he will not injure Don Quijote in defeating him (56.1006). However, the Duke's wishes are frustrated, for Tosilos, more comically than romantically, falls in love with the young woman, refusing to go through with the arrangement. He has so assimilated his role of possible husband that he thinks he has the autonomy to marry the daughter if he wishes:

> ... ¿Esta batalla no se hace porque yo me case, o no me case, con aquella señora? ... Pues yo ... soy temeroso de mi conciencia, y pondríala en gran cargo si pasase adelante en esta batalla; y así, digo que me doy por vencido y que quiero casarme luego con aquella señora (56.1008).

Apparently, as in the prose romances, there is to be a happy ending. The girl says:

> Séase quien fuere este que me pide por esposa, que yo se lo agradezco; que más quiero ser mujer legítima de un lacayo que no amiga y burlada de un caballero, puesto que el que a mí me burló no lo es (56.1010).

If only indirectly, the intervention of the knight is to bring about the desired marriage. We stated earlier that *dueña*-in-distress encounters in the prose romances do end happily, and most often in marriage. In the case of Dorotea and Don Fernando in 1605, the lovers were reconciled, although not through any effort on Don Quijote's part. There is to be no marriage in 1615, however. Cervantes now wishes to underscore the contrast between life and fiction. Don Quijote learns, upon returning defeated from Barcelona, that Tosilos received a beating for his impertinence in disobeying and defying his master, the daughter was sent to a convent and Doña Rodríguez back to Madrid. The actions of the principals led to the Duke's vengeance rather than to his good will.

Don Quijote, with all his good intentions, is patently ineffectual before the real problems of life. In following chivalric usage to solve a contemporary problem, he lends himself to another hoax of the Duke, and is unsuccessful in aiding those in need of assistance. It is of no consequence that he should attribute to enchanters the transformation of the seducer into Tosilos, or that he should refuse to accept the information the lackey gives him. Don Quijote's anger, although it centers on Sancho — "... eres ... el mayor ignorante de la tierra, pues no te persuades que este correo es encantado, y este Tosilos contrahecho" (67.1090-1091) — is caused by his collision with reality and failure. Tosilos has the same function in Part II that Andrés had in Part I. Andrés' disclosure of the results of Don Quijote's intervention in his life also occasioned an angry response from the knight. It is not mere coincidence that Don Quijote should encounter Tosilos during his return trip home in defeat. In pointing out his failure to him at this juncture of the novel, Tosilos shows the relation of the Rodríguez episode to the novel as a whole. The impotency of Don Quijote, who must always fail when he confronts real life, is underlined once more. He can solve the fictitious problems of a Micomicona or a Trifaldi, but in no way can he intervene in the lives of an Andrés or a Doña Rodríguez without damaging results. It is additionally necessary that Doña Rodríguez and her daughter should suffer. The *dueña* is punished for being so foolish as to fail to accept reality. The Duke alone had the power to force the seducer to marry her daughter. Having refused to do so, there was simply no justice for the girl. Rodríguez makes her continued presence in the Duchess' service impossible. Further, once the scandal had been made public, the only refuge for her daughter was the convent. [24] Her unwitting imitation of a literary fiction only worsened the situation.

The problem of Doña Rodríguez and her daughter was contemporary and related to the society in which they lived. There is nothing new in the seduction of a young girl, a reality in life and a universal theme of literature, treated by Cervantes from various perspectives on many occasions. What appear as striking for 1615, however, are the social and economic implications. The rich seducer, we are told, does not want Doña Rodríguez for a mother-in-law (54.990). Although Doña Rodríguez' social background is to be considered better than the seducer's, she is poor. He has nothing to gain from a marriage with the *dueña*'s daughter. [25] Cervantes presents a reversal of the situation of Part I, where Dorotea's wealth could not have been distasteful to her rich seducer. It is also possible that society's attitude toward *dueñas* might have influenced the young man. More importantly, the marriage cannot come about because the Duke will not intervene. He owes the rich farmer money, and does not wish to offend him. Doña Rodríguez brings the matter up twice. She is considerably more expansive in relating the story privately to Don Quijote:

> ... Aunque el duque mi señor lo sabe, porque yo me he quejado a él, no una, sino muchas veces, y pedídole mande que el tal labrador se case con mi hija, hace orejas de mercader y apenas quiere oírme; y es la causa como el padre del labrador es tan rico y le presta dineros, y le sale por fiador de sus trampas por momentos, no le quiere descontentar, ni dar pesadumbre en ningún modo (48.944).

---

[24] Leandra (I.51), her good name compromised by running off with a young man, is sent to a convent. As in the case of Doña Rodríguez' daughter, the scandal had been made public. In the cases of Leonora of *El celoso extremeño* and Leocadia of *La fuerza de la sangre* the scandal is confined to the knowledge of the family. The guilty Leonora chooses to enter the convent, whereas Leocadia, wronged and innocent, remains within her family until the time fate causes the seducer to marry her. In the case of public scandal, it was customary for the girl to be sent away to a convent.

[25] Economic differences are an obstacle to marriage between Basilio and Quiteria in the "Bodas de Camacho." Basilio almost loses Quiteria to Camacho because he is poor, but his ingenuity overcomes the drawback of his poverty.

She alludes to the situation again in 52.978, without going into detail, for the Duke is present. It is quite evident that continued economic security concerns the Duke more than justice. His earlier statement that as a knight he was obligated to aid "toda suerte de mujeres, en especial a las dueñas viudas, menoscabadas y doloridas . . ." (37.864) was, after all, only tongue-in-cheek. It referred to an ideal — both of fiction and society — he chooses to ignore when it is convenient to do so.

Looking at the matter from another point of view, Doña Rodríguez, a *dueña* who must make her way in the real world as a servant in a noble household, is in no position to expect that her demand for justice will be met. The contemporary *dueña*, a modest servant, thus contrasts with those other *dueñas*, noble ladies, who sought and received justice in the prose romances. Cervantes does not insist on the contrast. Apart from the obvious implications of the situation itself, the other servants of the palace are simply seen to resent being made to treat a mere *dueña* as a lady.

> . . . Ordenó la duquesa que de allí en adelante no las tratasen como a sus criadas, sino como a señoras aventureras que venían a pedir justicia a su casa; y así, les dieron cuarto aparte, y las sirvieron como a forasteras, no sin espanto de las demás criadas, que no sabían en qué había de parar la sandez y desenvoltura de doña Rodríguez y de su malandante hija (52.979).

When Doña Rodríguez steps out of her societal role as a *dueña de servicio* and into the non-existent role of *dueña de gran guisa/dueña menesterosa,* she steps out of her station in life, and so is eventually sent away.

The Doña Rodríguez story cannot be compared to other narratives in Part II. In these Don Quijote remains at the margin of the action, and characters with a vital anxiety do not appear. Basilio's own ingenuity, not Don Quijote's presence, leads to the "happy," or at least "non-tragic," conclusion of the "Bodas de Camacho." He is not allowed to intervene at all in the Claudia Jerónimo episode. Furthermore, there are no social conflicts in this story. Ana Félix and Ricote accept the lot handed out to them by society without psychological conflict (II.54.994 and II.63.1075). Doña Rodríguez, on the other hand, fights against the injustice done her daughter with the only tools her limited intelligence provides. She grasps Don Quijote as the only remaining hope.

To find similar conflicts we must return to 1605, specifically to the story of Dorotea and Don Fernando. There too we find a young woman seduced by a nobleman with a binding promise of marriage, and subsequently abandoned. The class difference (rich farmer's daughter, nobleman) also appears. In 1605 we find, too, a play between art and life. Dorotea, although idealized, is presented as a real person with a real problem. She assumes the literary role of the prose romances — *doncella*-in-distress — only as a method of leading Don Quijote home. With Casalduero, we might say that vital experience has been transformed into art. In contrast to the Doña Rodríguez episode, the problem Dorotea presents to Don Quijote has nothing to do with life. She invents a fiction, art. Don Quijote can resolve the problem only on a burlesque plane, in killing the giant of his dreams, much as he will solve Trifaldi's feigned dilemma by his flight on Clavileño. It is important that in 1605 Cervantes was able to find a happy resolution for Dorotea's conflict. Dorotea, with her intelligence, ingenuity and eloquence, is able to convince Don Fernando to marry her. Thus, in 1605 the social problem is resolved on an idealistic level, and is given the happy ending of fiction. In the ten years that pass between the publication of Part I and II Cervantes has matured as a novelist. The problem is found in a foolish old *dueña* and not in an ingenious young *doncella*. The protagonists are far from ideal. The story of seduction has been told from the perspective of reality. A foolish girl allows herself to be deceived, and the only individual who can make the seducer keep his promise is a nobleman whose best interests prohibit intervention. To her aid there come only a distraught and ignorant mother and a madman, who offers his "socorro" reluctantly. We cannot say that the Doña Rodríguez story has any true ending at all. We lose track of the daughter and of our *dueña* when they are sent away. Life goes on as usual at the ducal palace, and the Duke will have yet more tricks to play on Don Quijote and Sancho during their second stay at the palace. There can be no happy ending where there is no ingenuity, nor goodness, and where foolishness and error predominate. In 1615 we are dealing with the disillusionments and the pettiness of life. We could perhaps go further than Cervantes, and apply to all the characters of the scenes of the ducal palace Don Quijote's assessment of the "enamored" Altisidora's woes: "... todo el mal desta doncella nace de ociosidad, cuyo remedio es la ocupación honesta y continua" (II.70.1114).

The Doña Rodríguez story is neither sad nor tragic. Cervantes does not intend it to be. The *dueña*'s stupidity is too comic to permit viewing her as a tragic figure. The readers of the seventeenth century, furthermore, would not have been inclined to sympathize with a *dueña*. Cervantes himself has no interest whatever in the daughter, who is not even given a name. She is the "mala doncella" and the "malandante hija" in the opinion of the Duke and her fellow servants (979). Even Don Quijote is critical: "... le hubiera estado mejor no haber sido tan fácil en creer promesas de enamorados..." (978). Cervantes never approved of marriage imposed on a reluctant individual.

The Doña Rodríguez episode of 1615 stretches throughout Don Quijote's entire stay in the ducal palace. Events in the palace center around *dueñas,* with the dominating Trifaldi and Rodríguez stories. Doña Rodríguez appears from the very first moment of the knight's arrival and remains on the scene until his departure. The chivalric *dueña* who once populated the landscape of the romances no longer exists. In her place we find the *dueña de servicio.* The Doña Rodríguez episode is an illustration of Don Quijote's failure and the theme of literature and life. Cervantes laid to rest for all time the theme of *dueña*-in-distress by fusing it with the contemporary theme of the *dueña de servicio.*

BIBLIOGRAPHY

1. CERVANTES

COMPLETE WORKS

Obras completas de Miguel de Cervantes Saavedra, ed. Rodolfo Schevill and
   Adolfo Bonilla. 18 vols. Madrid, 1914-1951.
Comedias y Entremeses. 6 vols. 1915-1922.
Novelas ejemplares. 3 vols. 1922-1925.
Don Quijote de la Mancha. 4 vols. 1928-1941.

OTHER EDITIONS OF "DON QUIJOTE"

Historia del famoso cavallero Don Quixote de la Mancha, ed. John Bowle.
   London and Salisbury, 1781. 6 vols. (in 3). Bowle's *Anotaciones* appear
   in vols. 5 and 6 (vol. 3).
El ingenioso hidalgo Don Quijote de la Mancha, ed. Diego Clemencín.
   6 vols. Madrid, 1833-1839.
El ingenioso hidalgo Don Quijote de la Mancha, ed. Francisco Rodríguez
   Marín. 10 vols. Madrid, 1947-1949.
Don Quijote de la Mancha, seguido del 'Quijote' de Avellaneda, ed. Martín
   de Riquer. Clásicos Planeta: Obras completas de Miguel de Cervantes.
   Barcelona, 1968. 3rd ed.

2. ROMANCES OF CHIVALRY

Amadís de Gaula, ed. Edwin B. Place. Reproduces text of 1508 edition
   (Zaragoza) by Garci Rodríguez de Montalvo. 4 vols. Madrid, 1959-1971.
*La Demanda del Sancto Grial, con los maravillosos fechos de Lanzarote y
   de Galaz su hijo, Libros de Caballerías,* Part I, ed. Adolfo Bonilla y San
   Martín. N.B.A.E. vol. 6. Madrid, 1907, 163-338.
El Libro del Cauallero Zifar (El Libro del Cauallero de Dios), ed. Charles
   Philip Wagner. 2 vols. Ann Arbor, 1929.
Libro del esforçado Cauallero don Tristán de Leonis . . . (Seville, 1528),
   Libros de Caballerías, Part I, ed. Adolfo Bonilla y San Martín. N.B.A.E.
   Madrid, 1907, 339-457.
——— (Valladolid, 1501), ed. Adolfo Bonilla y San Martín. Madrid, 1912.

Libro del muy esforçado Cauallero Palmerín de Inglaterra..., *Libros de Caballerías*, Part II, ed. Adolfo Bonilla y San Martín. N.B.A.E. Madrid, 1908, 3-374.

"Libro segundo de Don Lançarote de Lago." Madrid, Biblioteca Nacional, MS 9611. Microfilm.

Le livre de Lancelot del Lac, The vulgate version of the Arthurian romances, ed. Heinrich Oskar Sommer. Vols. 3-5. Washington, Carnegie Institution, 1910-1912.

Martorell, Johanot. *Tirante el Blanco* (Castilian translation of 1511), ed. Martín de Riquer. 3 vols. Barcelona, 1947.

Rodríguez de Montalvo, Garci. *Las Sergas del muy esforzado Caballero Esplandian, Libros de caballerías*, v. 40, ed. Pascual de Gayangos. B.A.E. Madrid, 1874; 403-561.

La Tavola Ritonda o L'istoria di Tristano, Collezione di Opere Inedite o Rare, vols. 10-11. F.-L. Polidori. 2 vols. Bologna, 1864.

3. OTHER WORKS CONSULTED

BOOKS

Alighieri, Dante. *La Divina Commedia* [20th, 19th and 13th reprints respectively of the first edition, Florence, 1956-1957], ed. Natalino Sapegno. 3 vols. Vols. 1 and 2, Florence, 1967; vol. 3, Florence, 1966.

Alemán, Mateo. *Guzmán de Alfarache*, ed. Samuel Gili y Gaya. 5 vols. Clásicos Castellanos. Madrid, 1962-1968.

Arco y Garay, Ricardo. *La sociedad española en las obras de Cervantes*. Madrid, 1951.

Arthurian Literature in the Middle Ages: A Collaborative History, ed. Roger Sherman Loomis. Oxford: Clarendon Press, 1959.

Berceo, Gonzalo *Milagros de nuestra señora*, ed. Antonio G. Solalinde, 6th edition. Clásicos Castellanos. Madrid, 1964.

————. *La vida de Santa Oria, Cuatro poemas de Berceo*, ed. C. Carroll Marden. R.F.E., Anejo IX. Madrid, 1928.

Boggs, Ralph Steele, Kasten, Keniston, Richardson. *Tentative Dictionary of Medieval Spanish*. 2 vols. Chapel Hill, 1946.

Burke, James F. "A Critical and Artistic study of the *Libro del Cavallero Cifar*," unpub. diss., University of North Carolina. Chapel Hill, 1966.

Cancionero de Juan Alfonso de Baena, ed. José María Azáceta. 3 vols. Madrid, 1967.

Cancionero de romances (Anvers, 1550), ed. Antonio Rodríguez-Moñino. Madrid, 1967.

Cantar de mío Cid, ed. Ramón Menéndez Pidal. 3 vols. Madrid, 1911.

Poema de mío Cid, ed. Ramón Menéndez Pidal. Clásicos Castellanos. Madrid, 1913.

Casalduero, Joaquín. *Sentido y forma del Quijote* (1605-1615). Madrid, 1966.

Castillejo, Cristóbal. *Diálogo de mujeres*, ed. Joaquín del Val, according to the 2nd edition (Venice, 1553). Sociedad de Bibliófilos españoles. Vol. 31. Madrid, 1956.

Catalán, Diego. *Por campos del romancero: estudios sobre la tradición oral moderna*. Madrid, 1970.

La Chanson de Roland [252nd edition of the definitive edition, ed. Joseph Bédier, Paris, 1937], 2 vols. Paris: Piazza, 1964.

Chrétien de Troyes. *Les romans de Chrétien de Troyes,* ed. vols. 1, 3, 4 Mario Roques, according to the Guiot MS, ed. vol. 2 Alexandre Micha. 4 vols. Paris, 1965-1968.

Corominas, Joan. *Diccionario crítico etimológico de la lengua castellana.* 4 vols. Bern, 1954.

Correas, Gonzalo. *Vocabulario de refranes y frases proverbiales (1627),* ed. Louis Combet. Bordeaux, 1967.

Covarrubias, Sebastián. *Tesoro de la lengua castellana ...,* según la impresión de 1611, con adiciones de Benito Remigio Noydens, publicadas en 1674, ed. Martín de Riquer. Barcelona, 1943.

Deyermond, A. D. *The Middle Ages, A Literary History of Spain.* London, 1971.

Diccionario de Autoridades, facsimile of the edition of 1732. 3 vols. Madrid: Gredos, 1969.

Dictionaire de la langue Française, ed. E. Littré. Paris, 1874.

Dizionario Etimologico Italiano, ed. Carlo Battisti and Giovanni Alessio. Florence, 1951.

Entwistle, William J. *The Arthurian Legend in the Literatures of the Spanish Peninsula.* London, 1925.

——. *Cervantes* [reprint of the first edition, Oxford, 1940], Oxford, 1967.

Hurtado de Mendoza, Diego. *Obras poéticas de d. Diego Hurtado de Mendoza, Colección de libros raros o curiosos,* vol. 11, ed. William I. Knapp. Madrid, 1877.

Loomis, Roger Sherman. *Celtic Myth and Arthurian Romance.* New York, 1927.

——. *The Grail: from Celtic myth to Christian symbol.* New York, 1963.

Malkiel, María Rosa Lida. *La idea de la fama en la Edad Media castellana.* Buenos Aires, 1952.

Manrique, Jorge. *Jorge Manrique: cancionero,* ed. Augusto Cortina, 4th edition. Clásicos Castellanos. Madrid, 1960.

Márquez Villanueva, Francisco. *Fuentes literarias cervantinas.* Madrid, 1973.

Menéndez Pidal, Ramón. *Orígenes del español, Obras completas,* vol. 8. 3rd edition. 10 vols. Madrid, 1934-1953.

Ovid. *Ovid in Six Volumes,* II, *The Art of Love, and Other Poems,* trans. J. H. Moxley, reprint of the edition of 1939. London, 1969.

Quevedo, Francisco. "La visita de los chistes," *Los Sueños,* vol. 1, ed. Julio Cejador y Frauca. Clásicos Castellanos. Madrid, 1961, 189-298.

Riley, Edward C. *Teoría de la novela en Cervantes.* Madrid, 1966.

Riquer, Martín. *Aproximación al Quijote.* Barcelona, 1967.

Rojas, Fernando. *La Celestina,* ed. Julio Cejador y Frauca, 2nd edition. 2 vols. Clásicos castellanos. Madrid, 1966.

Rueda, Lope de. *Teatro completo,* ed. Ángeles Cardona de Gibert and Garrido Pallardo. Barcelona: Editorial Bruguera, 1967.

Ruiz de Conde, Justina. *El amor y el matrimonio secreto en los libros de caballerías.* Madrid, 1948.

Sánchez de Talavera, Ferrant. "Desir [de las vanidades del mundo]," *Cancionero de Baena,* vol. 3, no. 530. Ed. J. M. Azáceta. Madrid, 1966, pp. 1074-1077.

Santillana, Marqués de. *Marqués de Santillana: canciones y decires,* ed. Vicente García de Diego. Clásicos Castellanos. Madrid, 1964.

Las siete partidas del rey don Alfonso el Sabio, Partida II, vol. 2. Real Academia de la Historia. Madrid, 1807.

Suárez de Figueroa, Cristóbal. *El Pasagero,* ed. Francisco Rodríguez Marín, reprint of the edition of 1617. Madrid, 1913.

Unamuno, Miguel. *Vida de don Quijote y Sancho, Obras completas,* vol. 3. Madrid: Escelicer, vols. 3-9, 1968-1971.

Wilhelm, James J. *The Cruelest Month: Spring, Nature and Love in Classical and Medieval Lyrics.* New Haven, 1965.

Zapata, Luis. *Miscelánea, Memorial Histórico Español,* vol. 11. Madrid, 1859.

ARTICLES

Bohigas Balaguer, Pedro. "El 'Lanzarote' español del manuscrito 9611 de la Biblioteca Nacional," *RFE,* XI (1924), 282-297.

——. "Más sobre el 'Lanzarote' español," *RFE,* XII (1925), 60-62.

——. "Orígenes del *Amadís de Gaula,*" *Historia general de las literaturas hispánicas,* vol. 1, ed. Guillermo Díaz-Plaja (Barcelona, 1949), 534-537.

——. "Los Libros de caballerías en el siglo XVI," *Historia general de las literaturas hispánicas,* vol. 2, ed. Guillermo Díaz-Plaja (Barcelona, 1963; reprint of first edition, 1953), 213-225.

Burke, James. "The Meaning of the *Islas dotadas* Episode in the *Libro del cavallero Cifar,*" *HR,* XXXVIII (1970), 56-68.

Gilman, Stephen. "Los inquisidores literarios de Cervantes," *Actas del Tercer Congreso Internacional de Hispanistas* (1970), 3-25.

Klob, Otto, "Beiträge zur Kenntnis der spanischen und portugiesischen Gral-Litteratur," *ZRP,* XXVI (1902), 202-205.

Malkiel, María Rosa Lida. "Arthurian Literature in Spain and Portugal," *Arthurian Literature in the Middle Ages: A Collaborative History,* ed. Roger Sherman Loomis (Oxford: Clarendon Press, 1959), 406-418.

Wagner, Charles Philip. "The sources of *El Cavallero Cifar,*" *Révue Hispanique,* X (1903), 5-104.

Walker, Roger M. "Did Cervantes Know the *Cavallero Zifar?*" *BHS,* XLIX (1970), 120-127.